JANE GRIEVE

Slippin' on the Lino

JANEGRIEVE.COM.AU

Copyright © Jane Grieve 2009.

First published in 2009.

The right of Jane Grieve to be identified as the author of this work has been asserted in accordance with the *Copyright Amendment (Moral Rights) Act 2000*.

All rights reserved. Without limiting the rights under copyright reserved above, no part of this publication may be reproduced, stored in a retrieval system, or transmitted, in any form or by any means, electronic, mechanical, photocopying, recording or otherwise, without the prior written permission of the author.

—

National Library of Australia
Cataloguing-in-Publication Entry

Grieve, Jane, 1953–
Slippin' on the lino / Jane Grieve.

ISBN 978 0 9806 6740 0 (pbk.)

Family—Queensland—Social life and customs—1990—Humour.

Dewey Number 306.850207
—

Edited by Brian Clarke.
Design and illustration by The Letter D.
Typeset in Underware's Auto and Dolly 11/16pt.
Printed and bound in Australia by Griffin Press.

*For my Mum, Kathleen
(known to many as Lop)*

She was right all along

This to convey to you—Jane dear
The pleasure it has been to hear,
(via phone from my Toowoomba brother)
That you are now the happy mother—
And Robert father—of a boy—
The cause no doubt of mutual joy—
A son such parents well may rear
A modern type of pioneer,
Destined in future years to find
New routes & prospects for mankind—
Leaving the record of his name
Not "unsung" in our Hall of Fame—
That place no longer so outback
As when we started on the track
To find the words, the site, the dough
To get our project on the go—
And on the way to meet these ends
Made many dear & lasting friends.
Congratulations once again
And love to all from—Mary M.

PS: More difficult to find a rhyme
For Miller—Horrie, in his time
Not down to earth with flocks and herds
But up among those "Early Birds".

—Dame Mary Durack Miller—
Nedlands, Western Australia
4 February 1990

Contents

Dedication	3
Poem by Dame Mary Durack Miller	5
Acknowledgments	10
Foreword	14
Introduction by Hugh Lunn	18
—	—
Epilogue	178
PS: 9 ante portas	182
The Muse	186
My bit for Diabetes	188

1.	Motherly Advice	20
2.	Ms God	24
3.	The War Cry	27
4.	Snail Count	31
5.	A Lesson from Easter Dinner	34
6.	A Lousy Start to the Day	37
7.	Love Among the Ruins	41
8.	An Attendant Birth Pain	44
9.	Family Ties	47
10.	Lunch Box Blues	51
11.	Chook Power	55
12.	Slippin' on the Lino	58
13.	Rude Elbows	61
14.	The Iron	65
15.	A Gift Horse in the Mouth	68
16.	Fowl Play	72
17.	Bird Power	76
18.	Preth Five and Hit Enter	79
19.	The Kissing Gang	83
20.	Balloons	87
21.	Of Mice and Men	91
22.	Matters of Life and Death	94

23.	Fairy Interesting	98
24.	Life's a Bummer at the Tail End	101
25.	Veronica	104
26.	A Mother's Job	108
27.	My Perfect Boy	112
28.	Strangers in the Night	116
29.	Looking for Me	119
30.	All That Remains	122
31.	Bad Dog Month	126
32.	Cries of Snakebite	130
33.	Intimate Family Confessions	134
34.	The Animal Advocate	138
35.	Crossing the Mothering Divide	142
36.	Being Rubbished	146
37.	First Day	149
38.	First Day—Last Day	153
39.	Jock Saves the Day	156
40.	Melbourne	160
41.	Chaos Effect	163
42.	Confessions of an Easter Bunny	167
43.	Second Time Around	170
44.	A Brush with Danger	174

Acknowledgments

What, Brian? No clichés, no government-speak? But what would I be without them?
A writer, perhaps?

I have always wondered why authors make such a fuss of their editor on their acknowledgments page. Now I know. Brian Clarke has ruthlessly, and with great kindness and careful consultation, shorn government-speak and cliché from my work. He has helped me to rearrange weak spots and enlarge on strong ones. This book would be nothing without his enormous effort and bravery, and to Brian, my heartfelt thanks!

Thank you, Nick Bligh and Dan Pike, of The Letter D, for your wonderful composition and illustration. And Elizabeth Ure, my young support person, thanks for holding my hand from the beginning of this part of my journey.

To Julie O'Gorman at the Bethel Community Centre and to my Life Coach, Ros Loxton, of Great Thinking, who helped me shape my dream; my coffee ladies and dear friends, MaryRose Tranberg and Lesley Dalyell; my walking buddy, Michelle Brown; my *9 ante portas* women, listed elsewhere in this publication; my amazing network of New England Girls School friends; Lawrence Springborg MP, my employer of 16 years who says I write great letters in government-speak; the staff at Queensland Writers Centre; my Tuesday Philosophy Book Club ladies and many other dear friends too numerous to mention; my mother, Kathleen, and my beloved sisters, Sally Wright, Prue Graham, Tina Merriman and Nicola Potger. All of you have lent me your ears, support, encouragement and advice at one time or another—thank you. I love yez all.

And as part of the larger picture, there are some core people who have contributed to this particular aspect of my journey.

First, there was RM Williams, who believed I could achieve anything.

Then there was Dame Mary Durack Miller, who read my palm and told me I would be a writer one day.

Ken Cowley very kindly passed on my humble first effort at a column to Chris Mitchell, then editor of *The Courier-Mail*. I must thank Chris for having the faith that I could produce more, and regularly.

My *Perspectives* editor at *The Courier-Mail*, Shane Rodgers, encouraged me and taught me and congratulated me.

Hugh Lunn wrote on my program at an event, "To Jane Grieve, another writer, one I read—Hugh Lunn." You may well imagine what that accolade meant to me.

I have to thank my dad, Peter McCallum Paull DFC, for passing on to me his love of language and sense of the ridiculous; and although I know you didn't mean to, Dad, it was extremely ridiculous of you to die before my kids were born and thus deprive them of the great pleasure of knowing you.

To my husband, Robert, who begat my kids and facilitated my dream of a house in the country, a family of my own, a chookyard out the back, a garden, a few horses, some dogs, cats, birds, the odd snake, and lots and lots and lots of mice; thank you, my dear! It's been fun.

And of course, my kids, Sam, Lou and Jock, who provided the grist for my mill. Don't divorce me for this book, guys. I love you all so much and, while I fully realise it had absolutely nothing to do with me, you are great people. Dad and I are prouder of you all than you could possibly imagine.

Foreword

It's true—life wasn't meant to be easy.

Just don't say it in public, though. Former Prime Minister, Malcolm Fraser, left a bold legacy by so doing. But the fact remains that, well, there are some things that take you by surprise.

Like, say, parenting. Especially parenting, really. Before you find yourself in it up to the neck, you approach it with all the ideals of having experienced it from the other side—as a child. You clearly understand, from the perspective of the child you once were, exactly what your own parents did wrong, and loosely, but passionately, know you are going to approach it differently when the boot is on the other foot.

Then suddenly, in the peculiar way life has of seeming to unceremoniously throw you up on some isolated beach without your being aware that you were even on a journey, the boot is indeed on the other foot. And ye Gods, but it isn't quite so simple from that perspective!

The first problem is the lack of formal training for the job. For about the most important thing you have to do in your life, raise your kids into adults who are not bank robbers, axe murderers, or used car salesmen, there is no degree course. You're essentially and rather horribly on your own.

It may well be that you manage to stumble on some useful handbooks expressing opposing opinions about how to handle some of the myriad situations that are thrown up at you. It may well be that you are blessed with neighbours, friends and family who give you lots of unsolicited advice, some of it actually quite useful, but often from the perspective you yourself had before you found yourself in the hot seat.

But when the doors of your home close on you and your nest full of fledglings, daily and nightly, well or unwell, fit or exhausted, 24 hours a day, seven days a week, you are in the ring on your own. Centre stage, full spotlight.

The early days, when your child is a baby, terrifying as they seem at the time, are in fact but mild preparation for the reality to follow. You're thrilled when little Johnny learns to talk. Until, that is, he learns to repeat what he hears you say, whether or not you wanted him to hear; and then, to answer back. And then, worse still, he discovers (quite surprisingly early on, around Preschool) that you are not the bountiful font of knowledge he once believed you were and, horror of horrors, he starts to think for himself. And his thoughts do not necessarily complement your own or even come within their orbit, and nor do they necessarily fit within the parameters of the sanctity of your home.

The only training you have had is from your childhood experience, which is where your problems begin and end at the same time. And when occasionally you come up for air, and remember how you planned it to be, and decide to start over and do it right—well, life doesn't present you with a clean sheet of paper every time you approach it afresh. You have to trudge on with the blots behind you, part of your own personal story and that of your children. It is forever written in the psyches of your offspring, for whom it is merely a time game till they able to effect their dire revenge.

And another thing. A day dawns when you find yourself raging over something your child said, or roaring at him to get ready for school this very minute, and you stop and realise—I am my mother. Ye Gods, I am my mother! How did that happen?

O thankless task, parenting. A lifetime commitment, humour essential, hang on to your hat for the journey of your life.

It's true though, thank you, George Bernard Shaw:

> *"Life wasn't meant to be easy, my child,*
> *but take courage: it can be delightful!"*

Introduction

BY HUGH LUNN

It is always difficult, when writing about real people, to know when to hold back.
And it is an especially fraught task when you are writing about your own family.

Graham Greene, I think it was, said that, "to be a writer you have to be completely disloyal"—and Jane Grieve's incisive pen has not spared anyone.

However, despite spilling the beans on her family, Jane manages to make us find them all endearing.

Some of her stories make you laugh out loud: the uses of Coca-Cola and sandshoes; the history of toothbrushes; the disgusting doors.

And some stories—like JB Priestley's "little things"—are so to be treasured that they make you cry, and make you remember what it is to be a human with a soul.

ONE

Motherly Advice

What's this? Pregnant for the first time? Ha! Another lamb to the slaughter!

You thought you had spent all your years of adolescence and any adulthood to date, growing strong and independent so that for the rest of your life you could make your own decisions and cope in general, didn't you?

Wrong!

You thought you got an education so that you could READ about whatever you needed to get by, didn't you? Wrong again!

And you thought that if you needed advice about pregnancy, childbirth and child rearing, you would have to pay for it—you know, buy the book, consult the obstetrician—didn't you?

Heavens, no! Far from it!

All you have to do is appear in public with a bulging abdomen or a baby in a pram and whammo! People suddenly materialise from supermarket aisles or public seats where they have been lurking, just waiting for a person like you who obviously needs their unsolicited advice, which they give you ABSOLUTELY FREE OF CHARGE!

It's fantastic. It's a phenomenon!

It's a club and you're part of it.

Once your fecundity becomes manifest, so your body becomes the property of the greater tribe. Complete strangers now take a healthy, deeply personal interest in your once run-of-the-mill, boring tummy. Without so much as a "Howdy do", they rub and prod it, then ask personal questions that leave you reeling with shock, and wobbling off with the tatters of your dignity, thinking, "Who WAS that person?"

In hindsight, you can see that this is all part of being special when you're pregnant. It's the yin part of the yin and yang.

There's many an upside to being pregnant; but the public-property thing catches you completely unawares. You may not actually *like* strangers prodding your tummy! You may have this wonderful, indescribable feeling of intimacy with your unborn baby that you are reluctant to share! And you may have a fierce, maternal, protective instinct that makes you recoil.

But, you have to be gracious about it. Later on, you will find out that this is one of Nature's many little preparatory exercises. No, your tummy is no longer your own but, not to put too fine a point on it, you ain't seen nothin' yet. Just wait till you are getting around town with a pram!

Think how it feels to be a baby! Until you get used to it, it must be appalling! Enormous faces, belonging to people you (and often, your mother) have never set eyes on, bare multicoloured teeth at you at point-blank range. Halitosis or no, the mouths send forth a veritable symphony of strange, sibilant noises that mean zippo to you: "Sssssweeeeet!" they might say, tickling under your trembling chin; "How adorable, he's crying," (Hmmm. Strange, that); "Awwww, he's just like my little Billy," (Who cares?); "Now you be a GOOD boy now, woncher?" (Oh yeah, likely, just because you said so).

And then for Mother, the unsolicited advice and impertinent personal questions. "What sort of birth was it? Painful?" (Oh, silly question!); "Are you breast-feeding?" (I beg your pardon? And it's your business?); "Your baby's crying—it must be hungry!" (Nothing to do with your halitosis, of course); "Perhaps you don't have enough milk. You do? Well, perhaps your milk's bad?" (BAD human milk?); "Have you had it tested?" (Oh, please); "How are your nipples?" (Look, I'm going now); "Any cracks?" (I really must run along); "I used mutton fat on my cracked nipples." (I'm so pleased you shared that with me); "Have you tried cabbage leaves on your boobs for the congestion?" (Yes, actually, and my bra is stuffed with them right now).

To all of which you have to respond graciously or be deemed ungrateful.

Now, you ungrateful lot—listen up! Based on my experience, here is my free unsolicited advice for expectant and new mothers.

Being a new mother can be exhausting and overwhelming. Unless you have an amazing intuition for child rearing, or had heaps of practice on younger siblings, you will need a source of advice in order to cope. Get one good baby-rearing book. It is now your Bible. Join a mother's group, then a playgroup, so you can compare notes about your little darlings. Then look around and choose one mentor, someone whose own kids seem to have turned out okay.

This mentor may even be your own mother.

Whoever it is, be nice to them. You will need to refer to their expertise for, say, the next 25 years. And who knows, you may well become someone else's parenting guru in years to come.

TWO

Ms God

I have been up to the knees in nappies, and up to the waist in washing, and buried in the domestic paraphernalia of motherhood, for some time now.

This welcome (but somewhat stifling) circumstance has not, however, entirely doused the feminist fire that used to sputter in my breast as a single career woman, not all that long ago—or was it?

Now I am custodian of the developing philosophies of my three small children. This is quite a daunting task. There is so much competition nowadays from the entertainment market, which constantly bombards them with other people's values and opinions.

While I was hanging out the fourth load of washing on my working mother's Saturday just the other day, Sam (aged five) whizzed past with the straw broom.

It was, he happily informed me, one of his three boy heroes, all of whom could fly.

"What about the girl heroes?" I asked, trying not to sound shrill.

"Huh!" was his scornful response. "There are no GIRL heroes!"

Piqued, and lost for an immediate reply, I chomped on this information as I hung out the rest of the washing. Thomas the Tank Engine had already got pretty well up my nose with his team of subordinate, adoring female carriages following him obediently along and chiding him in wifely fashion for his wilful ways. Naturally, not having engines themselves, Annie and Clarabel and the gals would never DREAM of being as bold as Thomas and the lads, and actually *doing* anything except the occasional bit of nagging, or *going* anywhere except where their men took them! Gracious no!

Still smarting, I took my empty washing basket inside. Lou (aged four) was looking pensive over the playdough.

I could see at a glance that she was waxing philosophical, as soon became obvious. She was apparently pondering creation and matters spiritual.

"God must be very busy making people," she remarked, struggling to finish her second person before the playdough set hard. Timely, I thought. Very timely.

"Yes," I replied. "God is a very busy woman."

There was an utter, shocked silence from the playdough corner. Then, in a confused voice, Lou asked, "Mummy, is God a boy or a girl?"

"God is just a being, darling, neither a boy nor a girl. God is Love—a belief, an androgynous spirit, living inside people." Heavy, I know, for a four-year-old. But we don't beat around the bush with the facts of life around here. If you don't get in first with your point of view, without a doubt someone else will.

I snickered victoriously, but quietly, while I put the laundry basket away.

Meanwhile, I could hear some very deep thought grinding away over with the playdough.

Then, never one to be caught without the last word, Little Madam dealt the killer blow. "No, mummy, you're wrong."

"God MUST be a boy because 'God' is a boy's name!"

Yep, I certainly had some work to do.

THREE

The War Cry

It's not as if I haven't given it an honest go! Truly! I've done my best: asking around, reading, observing—even comparing—on the subject of kids, especially boys. I have to admit, I didn't know much about boys before this.

I've done so much research and bought so many *How To*, and *What Not To*, and *I Bloody Told You So* books about raising kids that you would think mine were the perfect textbook children.

Which they sometimes are, though not necessarily all at the same time or according to the same textbook.

I appreciate the basic precepts of acquiring knowledge. In today's world, if you don't know about it, you have no excuse. No excuse at all. There will be a book about it for sure, an expert with a blog about it, or a website. There is no point in sitting around complaining that you don't KNOW something. Information we have aplenty, thanks to the marvels of technology.

With all those trillions of people in the world thinking thoughts and discovering everything there is to discover, is there any hope that a dumdum like me could actually add to the sum total of human knowledge?

There must be SOMETHING new to find out, surely!

Well, I don't want to sound smug, but you may imagine my excitement when, by virtue of being a mother for a mere seven years, I stumbled on to something in this very category of priceless, till now unknown to humankind and therefore uncharted, rather bizarre and totally useless trivia. The Internet is FULL of that sort of stuff. But not *my* contribution—I haven't posted it yet.

Now, for nothing extra except a small portion of your time, all is revealed.

My discovery, because of the limited size (two) of my core research group, relates only to boys. But those two, being my own sons, I know intimately, and my conclusions are genuine, and earth-shattering.

I have discovered that boys ... well, some boys ... well, my boys anyway, are born with personal, distinctly individual war cries. Each is as unique as a fingerprint, yet all (well, both) serve the same basic purpose. And NONE of my parenting books know anything about it!

In my limited but finely tuned experience, I have discovered that the war cry acts as a complex warning system for other hearing creatures. This can be difficult for the hearing-impaired because it is often delivered with an impassive face and can be hard to detect visually. The distinctive cry, carefully crafted to send shivers down the spine of many a bolder parent than me, says,

"I am a boy, I am right here and look what I have done/ am about to do. Challenge me if you dare!"

It is used both pre-event as a warm-up, and post-event as a victory cry. You can learn to distinguish which is which by the tone of delivery (and often, also, by whether the noise, or noises, resulting from the activity it accompanies come before, or after the war cry).

One cry is a low warning growl; the other a kind of whoop, no holds barred—it's banned in the car.

As a parent, you must learn the difference so that you know whether to run for the child or the mop; whether you are in preventative or corrective mode. Whether there is time, in fact, to save the day, or whether the drama has already unfolded and you have to deal with the victim's tears.

Our two-year-old son delivers his immediately before a physical attack, such as pinching, pulling hair or raising a little hell with the family dog. And again afterwards with a different inflection if the operation has been successful.

If intercepted, the after cry may be just that—a cry. Boys don't like being intercepted. That's another thing I have never found in a book.

Now, our seven-year-old boy. His behaviour has been modified over some years of discipline (constant interception, perhaps) and maturity. His is milder. It often precedes or follows a corny joke, a jump into a muddy puddle which will obviously splash an unsuspecting bystander, or finding a chook engrossed in quietly, and peacefully, laying an egg.

If you are planning to visit us, I can give you our family code. Sam's is "Hubba Hubba Hubba." Jock's is "*Eebar. Beebar.*" Beware! These sounds accompany some pretty hairy forms of antisocial activity at our place.

Don't say I didn't warn you.

FOUR

Snail Count

Little boys are made of snips and snails and puppy dogs' tails; we all know that! It's a well-documented fact! All the same, I did not realise that this was meant to be taken literally. And somehow accommodated within my passion for establishing a garden. A healthy garden.

I love my garden. It's my outdoor escape. We gardeners love to plunge our hands into the soil of Mother Earth. There's a primeval instinct in a farmer's daughter to make things grow.

The Old Boy and I have developed a workable symbiotic relationship around the matter of gardening. I do the digging, planting, weeding, pruning, and pretty much everything else. He does the watering, from time to time, and claims much of the glory.

So between us, the garden pokes along okay.

And so, to our eternal dismay, do the garden snails.

Sam, who is a very small boy with kid priorities, has a

completely different attitude from mine towards the garden. He and I have a running battle of wits about whether or not snails are desirable in a garden. I feel VERY STRONGLY that snails are pests—absolutely no redeeming features. I regard them as feral, disposable, and preferably dead or elsewhere. Sam, on the other hand, regards snails as adorable little creatures, personal friends with fascinating personalities and captivating qualities. He makes it his duty to protect them from horrible people like me.

I, heartless, squish with gusto every snail I see. I reach into damp, dark places at great risk to my extremities (from spiders too) and drag them by the handful into the light.

Then with unsavoury satisfaction, I obliterate them.

Naturally, I am careful do this only when Sam is not around.

Sam, meantime, if he hears me snarling at a snail, or rejoicing over the discovery of yet another snail breeding ground, rushes to protect his poor defenceless friends with such heartfelt sympathy that I am made to feel like a mass murderer.

He carts them off and secretes them where they are safe to roost, or whatever it is snails do when they are not eating my garden, and breed where mother and other natural predators won't find them.

And having kissed and cuddled them for a while, and taught them a few tricks like "Show us you're alive, snail", he puts them in his pockets and carries them lovingly around. Sometimes his pockets absolutely bulge with them.

We have been known to discover, too late and with inconsolable woe, that a forgotten pocketed snail has travelled to the supermarket with us. The effect of this on the snail is quite devastating. And the inside of Sam's trousers pocket—well, you can imagine!

On these all-too-frequent occasions, Sam, naturally, wails and mourns his dearly departed friend. I, boringly, wail about having to deal with snail splatter on the inside of the pocket.

The snail saga has become an emotionally charged battle of wits and yet, in spite of my natural superiority (especially sneakiness), I am not entirely confident that I am winning.

Look! It's really great that TV and school are so proactive about encouraging the development of environmental awareness in our children. Yes, it's wonderful. Truly. We are on the same wavelength.

Tell me though, how do you answer a six-year-old, when you pull rank and insist that no matter what he feels about the snails, you are going to squish every one you see, and he says, "But Mum, if you kill all the snails then you might have a weed you don't want that only snails will eat and then what will you do?"

Oh, great. Who told him that? Does he really understand what he's saying? Or did he work it out for himself?

My kid's brilliant! But life and garden maintenance would be much simpler if he wasn't.

FIVE

A Lesson from Easter Dinner

I am watching and listening, as a mother should, and not intervening, as a mother is wont to do, while my howling three-year-old son tries to extricate his finger from the beak of an angry duck.

The child is the family baby. The duck is a family pet. Once a placid creature of prehistoric gait and a stern but amiable disposition, she has been pushed too far one time too many.

Not having personally had my finger in a duck's mouth, I am wondering vaguely whether, unlike hens, ducks actually do have teeth. I am also offering a silent prayer of thanks that it is the duck, and not the dog, that has finally snapped under the strain of Jock's constant tormenting.

There are a few issues at play here. One is the law of cause and effect, which says that this child has to learn, despite my telling him time and time again, that there is a limit to the patience of a duck or any other creature, including human mothers. That I cannot always be there to protect him from his own folly.

Another is my calmness when my small child is under attack, considering the unknown factor of the teeth and other, unnamed possibilities which mothers tend to think up and add to their bag of maternal torment.

As well, while it may seem flippant, it occurs to me that The Bard really had his finger on the pulse when he wrote, "What's in a name?" Because the duck which has a gruesome grip on my boy's finger travels under the misnomer of Sweetie Pie. Her companion, Mighty Duck, looks on nervously, overawed by such bold behaviour in a fellow duck.

A mere ten weeks ago, Sweetie Pie and Mighty Duck were delightful little balls of yellow fluff at the pet shop. They were so totally irresistible that they ended up at our place as children's pets where they were named for the aspirations of their owners. Now, truckloads of bread later, and from the opposite end of the growth spectrum, their names still sit uneasily with them.

Mighty Duck is the larger, but more timid. Sweetie Pie sports a rakish black patch on her head and won't take cheek from anyone. Both have morphed into huge waddling bow-legged creatures with insatiable appetites, incessant demands and disgusting bathroom habits. We have discovered another scientific fact in relation to the ducks. They have a kind of matter-duplicating mechanism inside them; it causes them to bypass the principle that *Every Action has an Equal and Opposite Reaction*. Opposite, yes, undoubtedly; but equal, definitely not. Much, much more comes out. And as certain as the fact that what goes into a duck doubles in volume is the fact that despite my reaction, their shit will end up on our back steps.

And so it is that some of us love Mighty Duck and Sweetie Pie more than others do. As they grow fatter, they generally fit most of my personal criteria for inclusion on the menu for Easter dinner.

But all this is beside the point.

The fact is that during Jock's tussle with Sweetie Pie, I, hardened by eight years of mothering, am able to calmly continue with the washing up despite knowing that my precious son is apparently (judging by the noise) being eaten by a duck.

I know that he is not in serious danger. However, when my first son was a baby, my softer maternal instincts would have propelled me out there boots and all, fighting off any small threat to his safety. As a result, he doubtless missed many an opportunity to learn by experience.

Given time, my evolution as a mother is nothing if not a series of giant steps. With it comes the understanding that kids have to learn to look after themselves, and can and should fight those battles that are within their capacity. Also comes the ability to judge how far their resources will stretch to do so, when to intervene and when not to.

It's a steep learning curve. The trouble is, no sooner do you get good at it than your kids have grown up and your skills are no longer needed.

SIX

A Lousy Start to the Day

One morning, one of my children (who shall remain nameless, but knows his name perfectly well) hit the jackpot. He managed to break all the records for creating mayhem during the daily wrangle to get everyone into the car in time for work, school, kindy and day care.

At the critical moment, as we lobbed everything into the car boot just minutes before we would have turned into pumpkins at the striking of the hour, he announced that he had an itchy head.

Moreover, that he had had an itchy head for absolutely ages and why had not I, as a supposedly caring mother, who should know by instinct that his head was itchy, done something about it?

He loudly and with righteous indignation proclaimed this minor discomfort to his small person. Yes, indeed I was responsible for all his bodily functions and, by projection, for whatever was happening on his head.

It was the first I had heard about it.

My gingerly inspection of the offending noggin uncovered teams of dreaded vermin doing gymnastics along strands of his unruly mop, their white athletic features offering an embarrassingly stark contrast on his dark brown hair. They were screaming to be noticed at school: "HEY EVERYBODY! YEAH, YOU OVER THERE, AND YOU, AND YOU—LOOK HERE, SEE THESE WHITE THINGS STUCK TO HIS HAIR? WE ARE *NITS*, YEAH NITS, THIS KID'S GOT NITS!"

His sister had briefly hosted nits during the previous holidays, but in far more discreet circumstances. Because we were away from home, we were able to keep this ignominious source of shame out of the local rag in our own district.

This time, however, discretion was going to be harder.

Slinging the baby into his car seat, I grabbed the child and hastily doused his head with foul-smelling stuff of great but dubious promise that was waiting fortuitously on the laundry shelf for just such a horrible emergency. Remarkably, I still managed to deliver him, hair suspiciously wringing wet, to school before bell time. For good measure, after school he was carted off to the barber and ruthlessly shorn.

At this point, it may be appropriate to confide in you, without expanding too much on personal detail but speaking from experience nonetheless, that head lice do not necessarily confine their perambulations to the heads of small children. Therefore, parents, be ever vigilant. This small disaster has the potential to get out of hand very quickly. Whoever you are, wherever you live, it periodically visits the eager schoolchild, thereafter viciously undermining the dignity and social standing of the entire household.

And if you are a new parent of a gorgeous infant smelling of Johnson's Baby Soap and sporting only a few darling wisps of hair, it is as well to be aware of the many and various delights that await you in the not-too-distant future; head lice are just one. In five short years, your baby will be mingling joyfully with the great unwashed masses, of which, naturally, *your* child is not one. The purpose in *your* life of the great unwashed masses is to have scorn heaped upon them when your perfect child returns to your immaculate home with something as unbelievably commonplace and disgraceful as head lice.

There is never a nice time to welcome head lice into your family. Our only other, to date, nit episode evidenced itself when we were in the plane on the way to Canberra to stay with my hyperhygienic sister, Tina. It was too late to request the pilot to return immediately to Brisbane, there to douse our shame in copious quantities of repugnant chemical shampoo which guarantees but does not necessarily come up with a once-only solution to your problem. We had no choice but to admit to our awful manifestation of gauche Queensland-style social delinquency in Canberra's airport arrival lounge.

Needless to say, we were adequately and severally medicated forthwith.

Don't be ashamed if you don't know whether your child is happily spreading head lice around the community. For a long time I didn't know either. Mind you, I would have been perfectly happy never to find out, but I am able to philosophise now, from the perspective of one who has survived thus far, that motherhood should be experienced fully if it is to be experienced at all. And while nits are one of the more bothersome manifestations, at least they are one of the less painful.

An itchy head is a dead give-away. If you genuinely feel you are socially above having head lice, then ignore this symptom, although this advice comes with the caveat, *at your peril*. You simply must not ignore, however, the eggs attached to the hair stems in the region behind the ears. They are horribly distinctive, only one possible thing, and clearly visible to anyone who has anything to do with your child at relatively close range.

Your chemist will have a good medicated shampoo and much attendant advice and sympathy. Follow all the instructions carefully, and lap up the sympathy. This may not be forthcoming from every quarter.

SEVEN

Love Among the Ruins

Motherhood. I came to it late, but I came to it with a vengeance.

Now as I glumly survey the ruins of my once nubile body (it was once, truly; not necessarily in living memory, but it was, once) I do some sums and realise that in the past seven years, it is only for the last six months that I have not been either lactating, gestating or both.

And that only because Jock had an obsession with gnawing, and an insatiable need to inspect everything in the room, including behind my back while we dined al fresco, which was playing havoc with my boobs. So I weaned him "early" at 10 months.

"I wish I could say that about my brood mares," muttered one of the die-hards at the race club when I imparted the seven-year part of this astonishing secret. It's all a matter of priorities, I guess. It makes me glad that I am not a brood mare. No, I am a modern human female and I have choices.

From choice, my lactating and gestating days are over, and while I don't want to think about that too hard, it's nice to have my body back.

The ruins of my body, that is.

Celebrating this momentous realisation, I returned to my weight-watching club. "Hello, remember me? Do you think you could help me get back to the weight I was when I came to you 10 years ago thinking I was overweight?"

Ah! Those seven years, after singleness turned into doubleness, and doubled again and then some, in no time—or so it seemed. What would my life have been without them? During that time most of my things have become "our" things, including my bed; I have not slept alone, and rarely with only the one person of my choice. I have scarcely slept a night through without someone arriving at the foot of the bed saying, "Mu-um, I've got the spooks; I'm sick; I'm lonely; can I get in?" Or if I make it through most of the night, someone in a cot beside my bed starts practising his vocal repertoire at 4.30am then stands up watching me for a flicker of life and finally, if I stay still for too long, hurls a teddy at me along with the magical word I once yearned to hear directed at me, "Mumma!!"

During much of those seven years, I wondered if I would ever enjoy the luxury of showering alone again. I did, eventually, but still the sound of running bath water attracts at least two people calling, "Me too! Can I hop in too, Mum?" So I have yet to bathe alone. I have yet to sit on the loo without an audience appearing out of nowhere, I have yet to find my toothbrush dry, and of the four possible phone connections in the house, I have yet to find one which is far enough away not to attract at least one or, at the most, three human beings from my immediate family saying, "Mummy! Mu-um! Hurry up! Can I … ? Can you … ? Can we … ?". And, of course, just when I have cosily secreted myself in a corner for a chat with a friend.

Socially I have still to have a conversation without constantly looking over someone's shoulder to make sure a small person is not stuck up a tree or running out into the road, getting lost or taking lollies from a passing bikie.

I have yet to come in here to write without someone popping their head around the corner and saying, "Can I help? Can I use the computer? Mummy! I need/I want/Can I have … NOW!"

Precious sounds. Lucky woman. Imperfect human. Sometimes I shout and rant, "Leave me alone!" But would I be without them? Never.

All the same, it is good to have my body back. The ruins of my body, that is.

EIGHT

An Attendant Birth Pain

Let's hear it for the classic understatement. Is there anyone in the world who has not had said to them at some time or other in their life, "Well, that wasn't too bad, now was it?"

You've just had a wisdom tooth pulled, or the leg you broke when you fell down the face of Mount Tibrogargan had to be set without anaesthetic, as a short-term measure before the paramedics arrived. Or you fell asleep doing a major, life-direction-determining exam, or you got married or divorced, or spent a night in jail. There's always some pathologically cheerful galah who will turn up as you are reeling from the shock and trying your hardest to be brave, and remind you with a patronising air of positivity that, "Well, (don't tell me your problems kid, but) that wasn't too bad, now was it?"

In my case, that cliché will always remind me of the birth—without the solace of pain killers, I might add, a gross oversight on my part (set my broken leg without anaesthetic any old day, I say)—of one of my babies. The child's father, doing sweet bugger-all, witnessed this momentous event on a date that became their shared birthday.

Perhaps he was feeling jaunty about the fact that it was his birthday. Although I suspect it was really because nothing in the whole process had hurt him in the least, except when I wrenched his arms from their sockets once I managed to lure him close enough to get a good grip on them. This small inconvenience was minor compared with what I was going through. He was very, very lucky his arms were all I could reach in my somewhat distracted state.

So when the worst was over, and parts of my anatomy far more precious to me than a mere broken leg were being reset, restitched, reconstructed and rearranged, he thought he'd fill a bit of air space with the world's oldest inappropriate cliché.

"Well, that wasn't too bad, now was it?" said he, with the air of someone who feared he'd miss out on his birthday cake if he had to hang around at this boring party much longer.

I was speechless. There are better ways I could choose to spend a Sunday than donning the dreaded backless white gown, I can tell you! Whenever I am close to childbirth, the prophetic words of a wise teacher I adored in my adolescence begin to strike an anxious chord. Among her worldly advice, most of which bounced off our ears at the time, her little pearl of warning went totally unheeded till brought forcefully and painfully to mind: "It is a pity about the unfortunate way the Lord devised for the bringing forth of children."

I have since realised that this was another classic understatement; however, her ladylike vocabulary did not include the use of the many colourful phrases I could, in the light of experience, now add.

Back then, blessed with the innocence of pre-pubescent ignorance and single-sex education, we were much more fascinated with what she had to say about the male anatomy, which was a mystery to those of us who did not have brothers. "There is nothing more comical than the sight of a naked man," she rasped, now with a distinct air of bitterness. Of course, as soon as her lesson ended, we all dived into our Messel science books to examine afresh the well-thumbed page about the male anatomy, thence to draw our own conclusions. And a certain undignified bout of girlish giggling.

But not everyone thinks it is a laughing matter, apparently. With our perfect family now complete, there arose the small matter of convincing the Old Boy that a vasectomy would be sensible. He was less than cooperative. In fact, one would have to say he was absolutely bloody-minded about it, mumbling incoherently about the possibility of contingent pain.

Dear me! I just couldn't understand his concern. After all, I would have been waiting outside the door of the surgery with these comforting words on my lips, "Well, that wasn't too bad, now was it?"

What more could he want in the way of comfort and support?

NINE

Family Ties

My friend Juliet used to say, "You can pick your friends—but you can't pick your nose or your family."
Juliet had a problem accepting her nose, even though like the rest of us she CERTAINLY had not picked it. But she had no problem accepting her family; she had not picked them either, but they were delicious and continue to be.

Juliet was lucky.

I'm okay with my family too. I too would declare my four sisters delicious, and pride myself in being one of their number. If only because they offer me a vicarious veneer of respectability.

Different! How could it be, when we were most certainly raised by the same parents, in the same house (I distinctly remember that they were there some of the time) that we could turn out so differently?

Just as I wondered at the time if I was adopted, because of a lack of baby photos of me, so I wonder now how I could have turned out to be such a shambolic person when, for example, my sister Tina is such a dainty, elegant little creature with an hourglass waist and shapely legs.

Everything about Tina smacks of poise and grace.

So, where in the family gene pool did I come from? Did I perhaps skip the civilisation part, and emerge straight from the cave? I have often wondered.

It was seeing Tina's peg basket that got me thinking about this just recently.

I am the sort of person whose clothes pegs are kept in perfectly discordant disarray. No basket for me! I keep them permanently attached to the clothes line, because that way it is quicker hanging out the washing. I am always rushing about, or so Mum says.

On the line, they take their chances with the forces of nature, including wind and water erosion, sunlight, bower birds and small children standing on each others' backs. When my pegs finally disintegrate and fall to the ground, they are left to biodegrade gracefully.

The fate of the clothes pegs is one of the few things, domestically, that happens gracefully at our place.

In stark contrast, Tina lives in a home, not a "place". Everything that happens at Tina's home happens gracefully. Whatever gene combination she received from mum and dad placed Tina and me at opposite ends of the domestic spectrum.

The clothes pegs that do duty for Tina, when not in use keeping immaculately clean, carefully de-wrinkled, laundered items in their ordained places like little soldiers on the line (left sock—right sock, left sock—right sock, hanky—hanky, shirt—shirt—shirt), are carefully arranged in neat rows in her peg basket. ROWS! I ask you. And I am not making this up. All their heads face north, all their tails south, they are efficient to handle and a pleasure to observe.

It's a bit weird. Such different attitudes to the care of clothes pegs, yet our birth certificates state the same parents and we grew up in the same home ... albeit me outside it, up a tree or down at the creek, and Tina inside looking after the dolls.

We share the same tidy, organised little mum whose pegs were always used only on Mondays—"washing day"—and in between times were placed carefully in the basket attached to the laundry trolley and wheeled safely indoors, there to be spared the ravages of the elements.

Mum's pegs lasted for years. Tina's pegs last for years.

It's hell being one of my pegs, quite frankly. And do I care?

My peg husbandry reflects the time and motion obsessions of a working mother. Tina's pegs reflect her calm approach to life. She's innately and discreetly tidy. Her possessions have a designated place, and spend a remarkable amount of their life cycles in it. Tina has the happy knack of creating a home. Her possessions know they are part of something beautiful.

When Tina tosses something idly down, it stands to attention, salutes, arranges itself harmoniously so as not to spoil the feng shui and warmth of the household, and cleans itself fastidiously at regular intervals till it can be of further useful service.

When I toss something idly down, it elbows rudely for room with its disgruntled and overcrowded neighbours, belches loudly and possibly farts as well, crumples into a messy heap with no regard whatsoever for harmony and serenity, and with every intention of gathering dust, and pretends to be asleep whenever I want to use it again.

I dunno. It's odd that we are so different. But our love for each other comes naturally, because we *are* family and have no choice.

I'm rather glad about that.

TEN

Lunch Box Blues

An issue, an issue, we all fall down.
"Issue", the buzzword of the moment, is a handy term, one carefully crafted to capture people's attention.

If you have a particularly good Issue it can take you far. Just start a blog, generate a support group and, with a little organisation, loud noise, strong leadership and fancy wording, hey presto! You get some government funding to pursue your ends.

If indeed you really want to, you might even resolve your Issue. Who knows?

I feel rather important, because I have an Issue of my own. I am inclined to get emotional about it because it is a morning one and I'm not at my perkiest in the mornings.

My Issue is quite simple—it's about kids' lunches. What on earth do you put in three lunch boxes five days a week, come rain, hail or heatwave?

Surely there are many others who feel as strongly as I do

about this daily nightmare? Other people, like me, whose pride won't allow them to discuss their inadequacies in the Imaginative, Healthy Packed Lunch Stakes, yet long for an easy solution.

Only once did I tentatively air my uncertainty to one of my peers. Only once, and that cured me.

I had sent my offspring forth to their respective educational destinations, and day care, with peanut butter and Vegemite sandwiches for about the 17th morning in a row.

Naturally, I had packed their lunches furtively, so the kids didn't see what I was doing, in the forlorn hope that they would have forgotten by the time they got home that they had been dudded again by their unimaginative mother. There is much to be said for being safely out of range at lunch time.

I chose another mother, Linda, who seemed the discreet and sympathetic type. With a quick glance to make sure we were alone, I intercepted her at the school gates. "What do you give your kids for school lunch?" I asked with a passing, you know, casual-like air, as if it didn't really matter much.

I hoped I looked and sounded very much like someone who would give *her* kids caviar and snow pea sprouts on oven-fresh bagels packed in mini-eskies. I tried very much not to sound like someone who resorts to peanut butter or Vegemite on whatever crawls out of the bread bin, day after day, and whose kids cry themselves to sleep about it and are considering divorce proceedings.

I think it was Linda's reply that made me realise that I could seriously be part of a minority group, not up with the times, with Issue problems. As such, I should undoubtedly seek out a Secret Society of Underskilled Parents and get some funding for a Lunch Box Training Support Group.

"Well," said Linda (and she looked like such a comfortingly ordinary person too), "I always deliver my children's lunch to them at midday, so that it's fresh. Sometimes it's salmon pate on savoury biscuits, with yoghurt, tossed salad and a fruit platter. Sometimes I do fried rice and deliver it to them hot but only when it's really, really windy and cold."

I am not exaggerating, and not a word of a lie. She would have continued to unwittingly demolish me if I had allowed her to.

Cultivating a dismissive and somewhat sneering air, as of someone who absolutely would not do anything of the kind themselves, I nervously interrupted with what evolved as a really, really stupid question. "Sandwich fillings?"

"Oh heavens no, sandwiches? Yuk, no! Not unless they're absolutely fresh and the pate is straight out of the fridge."

Fresh? Pate? I was shocked. More than shocked. I was blown away. When I was a kid, and I am talking about a decade when Linda was not even born, the sandwich-for-school-lunch mentality was total. No-one had told *me* things had changed. The variations were peanut butter, Vegemite, Marmite or jam, ubiquitously wrapped in greaseproof paper inside a brown paper bag. If you were me, you threw the whole lot out the window of the school bus at Connelly's corner on the way home so that your mother wouldn't go on at you for not eating your lunch.

As well, you always got either an orange or an apple that rolled around in your leather satchel and made all your schoolbooks smell like a fruitshop, a real gourmand's delight by the end of a hot summer's day. If it was an orange, you settled down to eat it on the school bus that afternoon, poking a hole in it with your finger and squishing it to suck out the juice. Which leaked all the way to your elbows, and sometimes even trickled down the inside of your blouse via your underarm, where dust stuck to it on the jeep ride home from the front gate.

And the apple, all bruised, stewed and inedible by bus time, you threw into the mysterious shallows of Oakey Creek at the Bowenville reserve. It bobbed and floated along with the current and turned up in your swimming hole just as you arrived at the creek for your afternoon swim. Which was a bit hard to explain to your mother.

I can see now that mum got off lightly. We NEVER had pate. We NEVER had bagels. The mung bean sprouts stayed buried in the damp blacksoil in the paddock and we had absolutely no idea that there was a world that offered something other than sandwiches for lunch.

Come to think of it, nor have my kids. Long may it last.

ELEVEN

Chook Power

Our darling neighbour, Dawnie, started our chook troubles.

Unsolicited, uninvited, and some may nastily say, unappreciated, she presented us with a small bantam family that was surplus to her needs.

We soon found out why. They had no respect for the law. Incest! I have to tell you. They indulged with abandon, and with no apparent consideration of the consequences.

Their capacity was astonishing. It was quite educational for the kids. Our bantam flock grew exponentially—because as you may well imagine, the rooster chicks quickly learned to do what roosters do, and did it. With their sisters and girl cousins and mothers and aunties.

Shockin', really.

It wore us out just observing.

We offered them back to Dawnie but she politely declined, citing—rather convincingly, and very firmly—a lack of room in her own chook yard.

We began to understand why there were local council laws banning roosters from residential areas. It's because of the sexual depravity. It never stops and children should be protected from it. So should council representatives because no human being is in the same league, not even Mick Jagger. Being shown up in this way by a mere bird must be very uncomfortable for council inspectors. So, roosters are banned in town.

Our chook yard was right outside our bedroom window. And we soon found out that roosters feel the need to crow the sun up, across the heavens and down again, with the odd little go at the moon. Not just once, and not just twice; roosters can't count. So they crow repeatedly, loudly and insistently, without due consideration for sleeping people and with exactly what in mind, no-one knows.

This, of course, is the polite reason given for their being banned in town.

We don't live in town, but we still had to consider us. The day came when we felt that it was time to take charge of the situation. The children were out so we had a cull. With an axe, wielded by the Old Boy, and with a very helpful excited dog in attendance. Roosters with their heads cut off were running around in all directions.

One extremely harried but self-satisfied rooster was spared the axe, along with all his sisters and mothers and aunties and girl cousins.

In no time, unaccountably, there was a population explosion in the chook yard; it was wall to wall chickens and broody hens again. During the day, they sat about in their yard looking vaguely sulky in the dry heat when they should have been laying eggs for our consumption. Or they sat about laying eggs, when they should have been desisting therefrom, with a mind to population control.

At night, they sat shoulder to shoulder on the roost, those that weren't broody, wings enfolding each other in a loving and altogether adorable way. The rooster, exhausted by his many labours duties commitments responsibilities and obligations, slept the sleep of the blessed, enfolded in a plethora of comforting wings, waiting out the night so that he could crow in the dawn. And resume his wearing daytime duties.

Setting hens glared out at small chubby people when they were sent to collect eggs with which the hens had no intention of parting. The same small chubby people wept and protested rather than do egg-collecting duty. "Thcarey," was the general consensus. Downright dangerous, I thought.

And it was absolutely full-on in the chook yard. An entire civilisation was living out its anthropology in our very own backyard. Fascinating.

We enjoyed visiting, and we enjoyed observing. But we were glad we lived in the house.

TWELVE

Slippin' on the Lino

My grandmother had a cook called Lily. My grandmother didn't cook, not much more than emergency rations, tea, toast and boiled eggs, so Lily or the Lilies of the world were an essential part of her life.

My sister Tina and I loved Lily, and were fascinated by her. If you sat under the big old kitchen table at our grandparents' home, Lota House, when Lily was cooking, you were sure to get some worthwhile scraps. And the comforting aroma of the Lota kitchen and the cool of its concrete floor stay with me still.

Apart from being a lovely, good-natured woman and the producer of delicacies, Lily had a way with her tongue, especially when she was rolling pastry or scones, flour all over the table.

Something to do with flour on her hands made her tongue dart in and out of her mouth like Nemo in the coral. In and out, in and out, in rhythm with her kneading as the dough got a thorough workout. Three tongue darts, then a break; three more, another break.

We could watch Lily for hours, staring rudely at her homely face with our tongues poking out. We hung around Lily and later on, played being Lily. We did the tongue thing, but it was never the same on us, although Tina was pretty good at it. Still is, 50 years later.

Then despite her decrepit state in our eyes, being over the age of 20 and perhaps 40 or maybe even 100, Lily got engaged. Her bachelor fiancé was called Patrick. So *Lily* became *Lily 'n' Patrick* to us kids, and we had two of them to love.

Patrick used to chuckle over the top of his fat tummy and say, "Well, eh, fancy!" in response to pretty well everything you said. It must have been pretty nice being married to Lily. And come to think of it, it must have been pretty nice being married to Patrick. Theirs was such a calm, reassuring house to visit. For us kids, anyway. Not the cat though.

Patrick had a cat. Or perhaps Lily had the cat, although my mother says she didn't. Whatever, when Lily 'n' Patrick moved abode into one of those gorgeous little cottages in Oceania Terrace at Lota, now worth squillions, the cat was a reluctant house-hopper. He liked Lily and Patrick alright—we all liked Lily 'n' Patrick—but Monsieur Moggy didn't like his new address, and he wanted out.

So after a few serious escape attempts, Lily did what any self-respecting and informed cat owner would do, living in a house with lino on the floor. She put butter on his paws. Then when he tried to run away, he slipped on the lino. No traction. That was the end of his escape career. You can't escape without traction.

Houdini was nullified, stultified, even de-moggified; domesticated, humiliated, deflated and most likely castrated.

I wasn't there to witness the butter method of cat control, but when Lily 'n' Patrick related the tale amid gales of laughter and Patrick's wobbling tummy, it had a huge effect on my psyche. I was never sure whether I was with the cat or with Lily 'n' Patrick. It must have been awful trying to run away and finding you slipped on the lino instead. What a horrible, trapped feeling that cat must have had! But then, he did get three square meals a day—with butter.

But for Lily 'n' Patrick, it must have been anxiety-provoking having a cat who ran away all the time, and who you had to worry about.

Then there was the fact of the butter and the floor and who cleaned up, and that was a worry as well.

It's many years since then and they have all become dust. Lily 'n' Patrick's lovely little cottage with the wooden footbridge across to the front door from Oceania Terrace has made way for a McMansion. The memories live on, though, in those of us who loved them.

Just lately, I am relating to Lily's cat. I've been slipping on the lino. Three square meals a day, but can't get any traction.

Shit of a complaint, actually.

THIRTEEN

Rude Elbows

Australians derived a lot of pleasure during the 70s and 80s from Larry Pickering's satirical political cartoons. Larry was famous for his rude—very rude—annual calendar, in which he featured 12 unlucky politicians of the day in their birthday suits. They always had spectacular attributes, lavishly embellished with ribbons and bows, which were a source of long-awaited ribaldry in many a household every Christmas.

Larry's concession to modesty was to carefully conceal all his characters' elbows. Elbows were the rude bits in Larry's world. This different view gave us all pause for thought about our prudishness.

But old ideas die hard.

My kids are going to grow up thinking that their mother had some kind of bent attachment to the clothes line. The greater part of my life since motherhood has been spent in earnest commune with it. Standing at the line with arms upstretched, then bending with arms outstretched. Sometimes both at once.

Yoga's *Salute to the Morning Sun* (or Surya Namaskar) was never this constant.

The kids always knew where to find me if I wasn't in the house indulging in some other form of involuntary exercise—exciting things like, say, ironing. Or vacuuming.

So there I was on this particular day doing my Surya Namaskar routine at the clothes line, deciding whether to excite myself by colour-coordinating the washing, or hang it according to ownership. Oh, *very* important work, with *such* an important outcome.

There were no sheets to hide behind, so the kids knew where to find me.

I overheard them down in the sandpit, sorting out who was to ask me something. And I instinctively got a sort of prickly feeling because I could tell it was going to be a tricky one, a rude one. One of those questions that every parent hopes they are going to handle with aplomb but knows that really they are going to spontaneously say, "Ask your other parent."

Nowadays we are told to teach our young to call a spade a spade. So many things were rude when I was young! But it's quite okay now and even desirable to give body parts their correct names and moreover, to discuss those parts and what they do as if they were, heaven forbid, quite ordinary.

Phew! It's a challenge for someone with a foot in the generation that did no such thing. Calling a spade a bloody shovel is just fine in theory. But there's nothing like a comfortable euphemism or two to oil the wheels of communication—especially with your babes. Prudish? Call it what you will. But I found myself sweating uncomfortably when I realised the first of such conversations was imminent.

I closed my eyes and thought of Pickering and his rude bits. I thought of my desire for some personal privacy—was it unreasonable? There was precious little privacy left with a young, inquisitive and eloquent family happily informing all who want to hear (and many who don't) what mummy said and what daddy said.

Oh, yes! We have learned the hard way that every bit of juicy information, gleaned both overtly and surreptitiously, will be cheerfully repeated when you are least expecting it—whether to the local padre, Gran, or at Show and Tell. How to monitor these indiscretions is another matter altogether. We haven't quite worked it out.

As I frantically pegged the clothes in an un-coordinated mass and waited, I sorted through my options. "Ask Dad," was one I seriously considered. Then I pulled myself together. "Right. I'll give 'em an honest answer," I resolved, squirming in anticipation.

"You ask her." "No, you ask her," went on for some time in the sandpit, with much shoving and pushing. In the end, size and curiosity won out and Lou, with Sam's propelling elbow jammed into her back arrived under the clothes line.

Without preamble, the question was delivered by the smaller party in the deputation.

"Hey, Mum, do girls have tentacles?" was the poser.

"Tentacles, Lou?"

"She means testicles," growled her pardner.

"Oh. Testicles. No, sweetie, girls don't have testicles." And then, moved by the look of disappointment on the little face I added, "We're lucky. We girls have those parts inside our bodies so they don't get hurt if we bump them."

There was a pensive silence. Then, never one to be caught short of an answer, Madam responded. "No, Mum, that's not right. See this bit here on my elbow? It really, really hurts when I bump it."

Aha! Larry Pickering's rude bits! So who's the prude now?

FOURTEEN

The Iron

I am interested and somewhat pleased to note that Jock has taken to his older brother's iron as a preferred plaything. Back when Sam was a toddler and I had room for emotions of this nature, I felt stridently passionate about gender stereotyping through toy selection.

These days, with three small kids, a home to run and work outside the home, I have to admit I am rather pleased with myself if I work myself into a passion about anything at all. It doesn't happen often.

It was the inverse of the toy selection thing that brought out the passion in me. I realised that, while parents were happy to force trucks and toy cars on their daughters, there was a certain reticence about dolls and prams for their little boys.

I talked Mum into giving Sam and Lou each a doll for Christmas. To her credit, she resisted at first, but gave in and got a job lot. Sam simply thought she had gone mad, in the way of old people, and left the doll to Lou's care. But I was not so easily put off course.

The day Sam acquired his iron was a day of particular passion. I can't really remember what brought it on, no doubt some domestic issue far beyond his understanding of adult expectations of each other in the ironing department, but that day I was determined that my son was going to learn that boys use irons too.

It was actually Lou who wanted an iron. "I'll get you each one," I announced. This sounded great to both of them while we were at home. Off we set to do the rounds of the toy shops. Toyworld didn't have one. "Mum, I want one of those cars," said Sam.

"No, no, son. I'm getting you an iron."

Woolies next. "Mum, mum, look! A Ninja Turtle sword! Oh, please! And hey! A Tamagotchi! Look! It destroys aliens. Aw, please Mum. If you're getting me something, don't get an iron. I won't use an iron."

"Sam, you are getting an iron," said his militant mother, her jaw set, her expression grim and determined. By this time, Sam was getting pretty peeved. Aisles full of noisy, mutilating, brutally aggressive and generally active material were slipping out of his anxious grasp.

Sam started to sob.

I have to admit, my determination did waver at this point. People were starting to look at us. And Sam was right—an iron DID look pretty tame in comparison. But hey! Toys are about learning, aren't they?

Things deteriorated. We were the noisiest patrons in Coles. Sam protested loudly and angrily. They quickly found a couple of toy irons just to get rid of us.

It was one of those occasions that so often seem to happen with kids. You start off with the greatest of intentions, and end in miserable chaos. We got home with two toy irons, one happy girl child, and the rest of the expedition party red-eyed and ruffled.

The irons got used, but not both of them for ironing. The one that ended up in the sand pit doing excavations for heavy machinery has now been rediscovered by Jock, who thinks it is perfect for roadworks.

Even if he does just chew the cord and whack the dog with it, who cares? I looked at him fondly this morning and thought, "Just look at that grip! Now there's a lad who will one day pull his weight with the domestic chores!"

At the age of one, they are so full of possibilities.

FIFTEEN

A Gift Horse in the Mouth

Ain't it just a fact of life that your kid would rather play with the box it came in than the expensive toy inside, for which you've just shelled out many hard-earned bucks?

Toy manufacturers MUST be aware of this phenomenon; yes, of course they are. That's why they mould the toys so firmly into the packaging in their boxes so that neither can be sold without the other.

Otherwise and without a doubt, once we parents have worked out that the kid would prefer the box any old day, we would leave the toy and just buy the box with the picture on the front. Oh, yes. It would have heaps of uses, limited only by the imagination of the kid! Think how this would save parents the heartache of sitting in the corner alone, playing mournfully with the toy of our dreams, while the kids play happily with stacks of packaging boxes and wads of wrapping paper, gaily choking themselves on the gift ribbon.

As happens every Christmas and birthday.

Take, for instance, three-year-old Jock and his wonderful new toolset. Just for our own pleasure in seeing his delighted little face on his recent birthday, we paid more than we could reasonably afford for a set of plastic workshop tools, including a buzz-saw that made wonderful noises.

The Old Boy was rapt. He gazed longingly at all those lovely little gadgets for ages, obviously itching to rip into the clear plastic moulding and hold each piece in his appreciative, handyman's hands.

In fact, it was touch and go whether he would part with it for long enough for me to wrap it up.

Come the morning of the birthday, the Old Boy was so excited! He couldn't wait for Jock to open his gift, so that he could snatch it out of Jock's hands and have a really good play with it.

We sat about, fidgeting with barely suppressed expectation and with expectant smug smiles while Jock started to open his gifts.

At three, this was to be the first birthday he would celebrate since he had graduated, with his siblings' help, to a state of conscious consumerism.

(Some unsolicited advice here: just for the record, for the first two birthdays in a child's life, a balloon will do.)

So we were excited. We were sick of balloons.

Because we were his parents and had paid so much for it, we secretly knew that our present would triumph, so we saved it till last.

The hour of truth had arrived. Everything was opened and critically inspected in its turn.

So what happened? Jock took off and pranced around the room, whooping with delight at being the proud owner of the cheap umbrella his siblings gave him, all his dreams fulfilled.

Then, while we sadly finished our cornflakes alone, he played with the empty toolset box for the rest of the morning. He was utterly absorbed. It was so insulting.

He then switched his affections to the neighbour's gift, an el cheapo toy bus. Weeks later, it is still a favourite.

Of course, pulling the dog's tail keeps him more happily occupied than anything else. (I should mention here that the dog is not so keen about this, but then it is impossible to please everyone.)

And the fabulous toolkit? Well, it's still underfoot but even the Old Boy is tired of playing with it. Occasionally, Jock will grab the toy hammer if it's handy and whack his brother, as the need arises. Apart from that, why use a pretend hammer when Dad's real one does the job of smashing things up so much better, if you can get away with it?

Why pretend with a plastic saw when there's a real one out the back that can take the leg or at least the sheen clean off one of the antique chairs? And without all that much effort either.

Yet again, we are faced with the eternal conundrum. Why didn't we think this through before spending the money? You would think we would have learned by now. We fall for it every time—bigger gift, bigger love.

Bigger nonsense.

A balloon, a hug and a good laugh go a long way, no matter what age you are.

SIXTEEN

Fowl Play

One day back in the 1950s, when mum was in the polio isolation ward at the Toowoomba General Hospital, her doctor looked out the window just as Dad drove into the car park. Our old Ford Customline was liberally splattered with a fortune's worth of black, sticky Darling Downs mud.

"No wonder you got polio, with such a dirty car!" he intoned sanctimoniously.

Oh, excuse me! Beautiful, clean Darling Downs mud. You could eat it!

Reckon that doctor must have been a pretty fastidious type. I wonder what else he did with his weekends other than washing, polishing, vacuuming and decontaminating his car?

Dad kept the Customline spotless, inside and out, except when it rained. He was pretty fussy about that. But us! Now, we are a different matter. Our old Holden, Silver, is the well-loved, well-used, not-so-clean sort of family car.

It seems like a waste of time washing her. I know that whenever I put her through the carwash it will invariably rain within hours, so that every pothole on our road fills with murky mud that has a mystifyingly magnetic attraction to metal.

Externally, a number of things adorn Old Silver that shouldn't—bird poo mainly, and often the bird as well. And mud, when it rains. Some things are not there at all that should be, like the car aerial, for instance, and one or two mud flaps. And a full complement of paint.

Silver's paintwork has seen better days. It comforts us to know, however, that in the course of the disintegration of the paintwork, Silver has helped to make a variety of farmyard fowl very happy.

Doc, our peacock, was once in love with Silver; she provided a perfect podium for his incredibly raucous farmyard sermons. And believe me, not until you have been woken by a peacock's dread wail in the dead of night do you know the meaning of the word "ghoulish". It is sheer terror. Once you have removed your teeth from the ceiling and a horrified silence has reclaimed the night, you find that most of the household, including the dog and the kids, have scrambled into bed with you.

We eventually got used to Doc's nocturnal calls. But the Old Boy never forgave him for wrecking the paintwork on the car. And Doc was a terrible tease. Hero, the blue dog, took a violent disliking to being taunted by him from on top of the car. When Hero shaped up for a fight, scratching the paintwork on the doors as he frantically tried to leap up and get at him, Doc simply flew off; it drove Hero mad. But one day Hero caught up with him; Doc's death was swift and violent. As he flapped mournfully past the car and up to the tank stand with the lifeblood draining out of him, Doc dripped blood and gore into the children's sandpit by way of, as always, having the last word.

But Silver, the Old Boy and Hero had but a brief reprieve. The guinea fowl took over the car podium and the role of farmyard tease. The traumatised survivor of a whole clutch of fowl who had been eaten by a fox one terrible night, he developed in his loneliness an Oedipus complex about poor hapless Silver (perhaps it was a colour thing), and finished off the paintwork.

No amount of abuse, physical or verbal, could break the bond. There he sat, in the ruins of the paintwork, mud, poo and scratch-marks his gifts of love. Such a touching scene! He was utterly devoted, to the extent that when we drove old Silver away, covered in bird poo and filled with excited kids cheering encouragement, he ran desperately down the road in pursuit, crying bitterly, till outrun by sheer horsepower.

And that was only the outside of poor old Silver. At the height of the "Kids Rool" era, anyone brave enough to get inside (and my mother was not) was met by a particular aroma rising from an archaeologist's delight of discarded detritus and disconcertingly lively flora in the back seat.

Sam, scientifically inclined, kept—and added to regularly—what seemed to be an entire rock collection.

The mound of clothing and toys would have justified a decent garage sale.

We once found a banana back there that was old enough to vote. And that is not to mention the rest of the contents of the fruit bowl, chewed and unchewed, that somehow made its way into the back of old Silver. And the odd biscuit, half-eaten sandwich, and, strangely, a baby's rusk, liberally sucked and misshapen, long after the baby had outgrown rusks.

Someone once found (although naturally no-one in our family put it there, since it was forbidden) a determinedly adhesive piece of chewing gum stuck to the seatbelt. (Household tip: a lump of ice applied to chewing gum makes it removable, even from hair, if you can get the owner of the hair to stay still long enough).

Several generations of spiders lived on the back window ledge of old Silver and were such a part of our family that the kids gave them names.

But in spite of the fact that we didn't clean the car all that often, we were really a very hygienic family. Honestly. We just had better things to do with our weekends. We had "a life".

SEVENTEEN

Bird Power

We opened up our hearts to the avian component of the household when the chooks arrived and in the fullness of time, even more birds came into our lives. Small ones.

Hector and Helen were lovebirds. They were a reward for someone who stopped wetting the bed for long enough to justify them (and resumed wetting the bed once Hector and Helen were irrevocably installed on our kitchen table and in our lives, and everyone was able to relax again).

We considered calling them Frankie and Johnny at first but the Iliad won out, and Hector and Helen they were.

Or was it Helen and Hector? Or perhaps, actually, Hector and Hector, or Helen and … oh well, you get the picture. Their desire was more discreet than the chook yard saga, and no progeny, but the foreplay was almost as engaging.

Apart from the constant seed droppings on the kitchen floor, we grew to love Hector and Helen. And we fondly believed they grew to love us.

Then a cataclysmic thing happened. Suddenly, shockingly, and probably aided and abetted by small chubby people, Helen escaped from captivity (or was it Helen who stayed and Hector who left?). This left Hector (or Helen)—and the small chubby people—bereft. So to compensate we began to shut up the kitchen tightly to avoid any further catastrophes, and let Hec/elen out of the cage regularly to join us at breakfast. He/she familiarised himself/herself with the kitchen. He/she proved an avid and adventurous explorer, falling into jugs, coffee cups and the goldfish bowl. Then he/she forgot about us, and established a camp high up in the top of a cupboard, among some obsolete crockery.

How quaint, we thought.

He/she seemed to have an obsession with time, because he/she would flit to the kitchen wall clock, sit there to catch his/her breath and poo on it a few times, and then fly over and sit pecking idly (we thought) at the calendar hanging from a hook on the wall, returning laden with small pieces of calendar to the hideout in the cupboard.

How cute, we thought.

Then the calendar began to fall apart. For several weeks we missed important appointments and forgot which day it was, even what month, because slowly the calendar leaves flipped back all the way to the beginning of the year under the ministrations of H's obsession.

Then things started to get nasty. Hec/elen's personality changed. He/she got cranky. He/she began to fluff up with rage and bite our fingers when we approached him/her to put him/her back into his/her cage. He/she began to intimidate us by swooping low over our heads as we ate our breakfast.

We were never quite certain, but it is possible that he/she even shat in our cornflakes, a very spiteful act considering, and one that began to tip the scales of justice and equity.

The situation reached a pitch, and became intolerable, when he/she chased one of the ducklings (yes, ducklings too. You have to experience pets fully or you haven't been a proper parent) around the kitchen floor with a ferocity that belied his/her size. Then he/she drew blood on poor little Sweetie Pie's nose.

Enough was enough. We decided that Hec/elen was frustrated.

A marriage was arranged that was unique in the history of the world. Our bird was carted off to the pet shop for a formal sex determination before a final decision could be made as to whether he/she actually required a bride or a groom.

Turns out Hector was a girl. We got her a groom (well, we think it was a groom; the lady in the pet shop was not completely certain) but the new love story did not go much further anyway.

One of them went ballistic. Things got cannibalistic. And in no time at all we were back to having just the one lovebird again. A rather fat one.

It was disgusting, actually. Disgusting and very, very disappointing.

EIGHTEEN

Preth Five and Hit Enter

My four-year-old son thinks it is complete nonsense that anyone his age ever believed that the moon was made out of cheese. No-one could be tho thilly, he snorts.

Not that I am going to ruin his life and mine by admitting this to him, but until she was quite a bit older than four, his own mother used to believe the moon was made out of cheese.

For ages she was certain also that the shadowy thing on the moon you can still see on it all these years later, unchanged despite the passage of vast aeons of time, the hole in the ozone layer, pollution and climate change, was actually a very large, cheese-eating rabbit.

Those were quite reasonable things to believe when I was young. Everyone encouraged such expressions of innocence as being delightfully quaint. Children's books reinforced these concepts and added a large number of enchanting fairy-tale myths to titillate the young imagination; myths that took a great deal of unravelling as bland reality gradually encroached on my wistful imaginings with the unfolding of time.

Real life was actually much more boring than that.

Of course, now I am grown up I know about most stuff; almost as much as my kids, I am sometimes bold enough to think. But then, none of them is yet ten. And on clear nights, I still wonder ... what *is* that on the moon, if it's not a rabbit?

That's the trouble these days; IT and Sesame Street have turned our kids into such pompous little know-it-alls. You can't put anything over them; it's no fun anymore. You're never sure that you are one step ahead, and you are uneasily certain that the deception won't last for long anyway. The mysteries of the natural world are presented to them exactly as they are.

To be quite honest, I do prefer the modern approach. I just wish I knew as much as my kids do, that's all.

So complete was our technological ignorance in the dim dark days of my youth that my mother's cleaning lady was outraged the day of the first moon landing. She considered the whole thing an enormous hoax and a personal affront to her intelligence.

The NASA broadcast of Mankind's Great Moment happened on cleaning day. Everyone knocked off working on the farm to watch on TV.

Their field of vision was spasmodically obscured by Mrs D who, infuriated, jabbed her broomstick at the screen with the passion of a woman who was not going to be made a fool of. As they sat riveted to the set, Mrs D, unimpressed with the whole thing and feeling it did not rate more than a short pause in her labours, swept around them noisily.

As Neil Armstrong took those first bouncy steps on the moon, Mrs D paused, leaned on her broom and watched grimly. Then suddenly, she tossed her head, let out a gruff "Humph!" and resumed her vigorous sweeping. "I don't see how they can land on the moon this week anyway. It's not even full!" she snorted with disgust.

You wouldn't put that one over anyone over the age of three nowadays. Not that I would ever admit to my kids that I had been sort of wondering whether it was cheese those astronauts were putting in their collecting bags that day.

I can handle a little derision from my kids about growing up in an era when ignorance was simply a lack of available scientific knowledge, or related to the child-raising mores of the day. But what really gets me is how kids just "get it" as far as computer technology is concerned. I don't. It's not fair.

Nothing about computers bothers my kids. I still have to help them do up their shoelaces and one of them can't be trusted to wipe his backside properly, but I have to go to them for help if I want to do anything slightly fancy, like download some photos, or upgrade my firewall.

And I simply have no desire to understand their computer games.

But like all good things, early computer skills can go too far. The other day Lou Lou, aged seven, was playing school marm to the four-year-old who reckons he knows everything about the moon. An old pair of glasses balanced on her nose, she had him seated at the play desk with pencil poised.

"And now, children. How do you write 'five'?" asked Teacher.

"Preth 5 and hit enter," was his spontaneous reply.

Obviously a sign of the times.

NINETEEN

The Kissing Gang

What's in a kiss?

A kiss says it all. Well, for most people it does. Not for Eskimos and Maoris perhaps, but seriously—who wants to rub noses?

So, Eskimos and Maoris aside, we all love kisses. Don't we?

Well? Don't we?

Apparently, no. There's us as love kisses, and then there are small boys.

Most parents who collect their kids after infant school would agree that the post-school routine in the car on the way home can be fraught with emotion. It varies according to everybody's (including the parent's) current frame of mind, level of stress/hunger/fatigue and general personal comfort.

In our car, it is usually a gruesome time of day. For starters, I am exhausted from a day at work, so I am not at my most patient. For the kids, all the pent-up emotion from the strain of behaving well within eye- and earshot of Mrs Keevers and Mrs Mac is at boiling point by 3.00pm. It can be quite difficult, if not downright impossible, to have a civilised conversation in our old Silver car on the way home. Let alone chat about what everyone's been doing.

Five days a week, you drop your kid off at 8.30am and don't see them again till 3.00pm. You know very little about a large chunk of their daily lives. So, although it's like drawing teeth, you tend to probe.

I'm fairly cautious. Our typical afternoon's exchanges go something like this: "How was school today, Sam?" Reply: "Okay."

"Oh. Right."

Then, brightly, "And how about you, Lou?"

"Fine, Mummy, but why can't I have a lolly? You never let me have sweets! Lucy gets sweets IN HER LUNCH BOX and all I want is some bubblegum I won't get it in my hair or on the car seat that wasn't me who got chewing gum stuck to the seatbelt PLEASE can I have some why not? Waaaaaagh!"

So, blocked at every turn, and according to my current frame of mind, level of stress/hunger/fatigue, I either blow my top, resort to more assertive tactics (like: "Well then, who did you *play* with today?"), or I retreat, defeated.

Recently Sam gave me a rare treat—a spontaneous answer, first up, and a variation on the usual theme.

"How was your day, Sam?"

"AWFUL."

"Oh my! Gracious! Why was it awful?"

(Shudders of masculine revulsion). "I got caught by the Kissing Gang."

The grim story unfolded. The Kissing Gang has been operating for almost a year; with, I might add, an abysmal success rate. It consists of three seven-year-old girls united with one thing on their minds; to catch a boy and kiss him. To Sam at age seven, being caught and kissed by a girl is a fate worse than anything life could throw at him. It's repulsive. It's ghastly. It's ... well, it's worse than being caught out accidentally sticking bubblegum to the seatbelt. "Did they kiss you?"

"No way! They weren't quick enough. They haven't kissed anyone yet except a Year One kid. Oh, and their mothers."

Obviously he was very shaken. It was a near thing, but he fought strenuously and came up trumps—and unkissed.

I couldn't help being shocked at how things had changed since my day.

I would never have let a catch like Sam get away without landing at least one kiss on him. Even an air kiss.

Bowenville State School was quite small in the early '60s. I operated successfully as a lone female predator, although I relied heavily on back-up troops. To me, there was one and only one entirely kissable boy in my class—he was, in fact, the only boy in my class. Stuart Westerman. To hear his name still makes my heart quicken. He, like Sam, was a very unwilling recipient of my affections. I had to deputise a few older and sturdier boys to throw him to the ground whenever I needed to plant one on him.

In hindsight, having seen more of the world, I now realise that his reaction was not unlike that of a bull calf at branding time. After being thrown and kissed, Stuart would scramble up, shake the dust and loose grass from his Bowenville State

School uniform and bolt as fast as he could in any direction so he could recover in a place where I was not. It was rather insulting really.

I persisted undaunted though, perhaps sensing that this was a parallel to real life; and I have since learned that in some respects, it was.

TWENTY

Balloons

In a world full of change, it is great when some things remain the same. The basic article, anyway, even if the packaging grows more sophisticated.

Take Iced VoVos, for example. I always leap at them. They have such wonderful connotations for me, back to long-ago birthdays when something fancier than home-cooked biscuits was called for.

I get nostalgic when I see an Arnott's Nice biscuit with sugar sprinkled on top, or an Arnott's Milk Arrowroot. Those two timeless favourites were the fancy items when Lily the cook brought morning tea for my grandmother, Mimi, on the verandah at Lota when I was young. Oh, how we had to restrain ourselves as we waited for Mimi to offer us one. No jiggling impatiently on the straw verandah chair. We tried so hard to sit still and Be Good, and when we got one, not to drop crumbs.

And of course, if you accidentally said a rude word like

"damn", you had no hope of getting a biscuit at all.

These are some of my earliest vivid memories. There we would sit, my sisters and I, in our pretty dresses, nibbling our Iced VoVos. Everyone else always managed to be gooder than me, as we looked out over Moreton Bay where the marina is now, to Stradbroke Island, which I firmly believed was England.

I used to go back to the Bowenville State School, way inland on the Darling Downs, and brag to my classmates (many of whom had not even seen the sea, more than 200 kilometres away and very distant then to those without a car or a grandmother at the seaside) that I had seen England.

Iced VoVos, Nice biscuits, Milk Arrowroots, and balloons. Four constants that have come with me all the way from childhood.

Balloons haven't changed. Balloons still mean happiness. Balloons mean birthdays and Christmas, kids, parties and fun. Balloons mean spooking the stuffing out of generations of dogs when they go bang; they mean those same juicy, immensely disgusting noises we used to make, that our kids make now to shock us and think are new.

Think balloons, think memories. Those long-term memories are easier to dig up, while the short-term ones seem to evaporate. One balloon memory I have is of my sister Tina, when she was about six. This was her "scientific experiment", and with intense concentration, she stuck a pin into a balloon. She had been so sure that the air would go out very slowly from such a very small hole.

Well, the bang took 10 years off her life, and completely ruined that birthday party. Tina was that sort of little girl;

scientifically inclined. She had her own way of thinking things through.

Balloons are still made out of the same old rubbery stuff, in the same old basic colours (maybe a few more), filled with air, and used in the same old way. Or are they?

One night at bedtime Sam, aged seven, said, "I bet Lou's balloon is far, far, far away on the other side of the universe by now, Mum."

"Yeah, Mum," Lou, aged five, joined in eagerly. "I bet it's billions and billions of miles away by now."

"Mmmmmmm," I said, delving into my shrivelled hippocampus for possible clues as to which balloon, which occasion, and which scientific phenomenon might have set a balloon to doing such a thing.

Was it the last birthday, Lou's, which was months ago? And did we actually have balloons at Lou's party? Well, of course we did. But was there something particular I should recall about Lou's balloon?

Recognising the familiar glazed expression in my eyes, Sam encouraged me with, "Don't you remember, Mum? When Lou was three and she lost her helium balloon at the Gold Coast and she was so upset Dad had to go back and buy her another one!"

Ye gads! Did we go to the Gold Coast when Lou was three? I don't remember. Am I expected to remember back two years? "It only takes four days to get to the moon, Mum. How many days since Lou was three? That helium balloon must be way, way past the moon by now, Mum, absolutely miles across the universe. That is, if it hasn't popped. It was made out of mighty strong stuff. Do you think it would have popped by now, Mum?"

How on earth would I know? When I grew up, the earth was flat. The moon had a man in it, although it looked more like a rabbit. And balloons were filled with air out of your lungs, not helium; they died an untimely death at the hands of some small child, and went out with the rubbish. It never occurred to anyone, not in our household anyway, that they might end up on an intergalactic expedition.

Ah! But in a world full of possibilities, you just never know what might happen.

TWENTY-ONE

Of Mice and Men

One day our hay supplier found a hairless, sightless, motherless baby mouse amongst a load of hay he delivered.

To our great and unmitigated horror, which, of course, as caring parents we hid cleverly, he very kindly gave it to Sam.

Sam, who was six at the time, was thrilled with his new pet.

It exhibited very few signs of life, but was easy to manage and cart around, didn't seem to make any mess or show any tendency to want to get into the bread bin and sort through the choicest bits of tomorrow's toast, and so we generously allowed him to keep it.

We all know who ends up looking after the family pets. So in no time I, resident rodent-hater, was until nature took its course, on the hour every hour feeding this tiny scrap of tenuous existence with droplets of soy milk on the end of a sliver of matchstick. The poor little creature sucked and then rubbed its adorable little muzzle and sightless little eyes, before resuming its completely inert attitude on its bed of cotton wool.

You could see every tiny, perfectly formed rib on its little rib cage; its tiny little paws clung to your finger so pathetically and trustingly as it sucked its milk, its little whiskers quivering and its bare little gums trembling. Oh, that overwhelming feeling of wanting to protect something so completely dependent on you alone (yes, forget about its owner, who had lost interest and was playing cars immediately he realised that this was not an action pet!).

It did rather tug at my maternal heartstrings.

However, I'd prefer that no-one told our neighbour, Gai, about this. Gai is our neighbourhood Cooch Windgrass, viz. indiscriminate animal lover and keeper of useless pets that demand and receive her time, attention and hard-earned bucks. Gai is not a strident animal advocate, but her spontaneous loving is heartwarming to behold. And puts you to shame for even considering setting a mouse trap.

Every neighbourhood should have a Gai, to stoke the fires of human compassion from time to time.

One day our Gai found a family of RATS, no less, at the bottom of a 44-gallon drum. I mean, RATS! Ugh!

Knowing that the responsible thing to do during the worst rodent plague in living memory was to dispatch them to rodent heaven, (or to put it in the vernacular, get rid of the bloody awful things) and unable to do such a dastardly thing herself, she called on a neighbour to help her out. When that more pragmatic remover of pests arrived, he found Gai wringing her hands as she peered anxiously over the edge of the 44-gallon drum, while the rats were lolling around, relaxed, and enjoying a Last Supper of delectable morsels and drink provided thoughtfully by Gai.

They were no doubt also planning their next moonlight raid on Gai's pantry.

The thought of this homey little tableau had, until the arrival of our own orphaned mouse, provided us and ours with quite a bit of merriment at Gai's expense. And now, here was I, beholden to the same rat and mouse plague next door, held to ransom by Gai's rats' smelly, despicable, promiscuous mouse cousins, who got into bed with us and chewed the hairs on our very heads. Yet despite this, my unquenchable maternal instinct still made me guilty for a day of not only harbouring, but also nurturing a baby mouse. So tiny and defenceless! So trusting and dependent! Yet with such potential for a promising future career in chewing hairs on unsuspecting, prone bodies and getting into the biscuit tin and the linen cupboard and worse, my underwear drawer.

Alas, I was not a good foster mother. Nature did not intend for such delicate creatures to be separated from their mummy's milk and warm body. Sam's little pet quietly slipped off into limbo where by now it has, no doubt, met up with Gai's rats, grown up and is having an absolute ball chewing at the electrical wiring in Heaven.

TWENTY-TWO

Matters of Life and Death

In the pre-dawn darkness, an anxious whisper wafts shakily from its owner's temporary nest in the comfy depths of our king-sized water bed.

"Mum," it says, "are we going to eat the cat?"

Piccaninny dawn is the cogitative time for our son, Jock. While his brain is booting up for the day, matters of significance in his small world are regurgitated, chewed over, tossed about for a while, discussed with his parents, and then digested.

There is a lot of strange stuff to grapple with at the age of three, especially when such sophisticated issues as the extinction of dinosaurs, the mortality of loved ones, including the cat, and the concept of being liked are burning his brain.

This is a story—which may be distressing for some readers—of pets, country living and semi-subsistence. It is a story of do-it-yourself in a normal omnivorous lifestyle (you're *not* going to cut those leaves off my spinach plant are you, Mum?), necessity, duck poo on the back steps, and a garden wilfully destroyed by pet pigs.

The pet part of the tale relates mostly to me. Try offering me a pet of some kind for my dear children! There's plenty of room on your acreage, and no council regulations or fussy neighbours to bother you, you might say (as my children do) to persuade me.

"No thanks, I'm pretty well set up for pets," will be the prompt response from this battle-hardened player in the game of motherhood.

You are, after all, dealing with a mother who, overjoyed by the prospect of living on acreage, has adopted over the years, for the delight of her children, a complete inventory of pets. We have so far hosted (and loved) two matched pairs of bantams, two guinea pigs, a pair of lovebirds, two dogs, several guinea fowls, two peacocks, a pair of ducks, numerous cats (each replacing the cat before, and each quickly dispatched by Hero, the blue cattle dog), other creatures long forgotten, and most recently, a pair of adorable and irresistible pink piglets.

All of these God's creatures have similarities. As they grow larger, they lose their appeal as little playthings. They eat copiously, follow me around, and collectively make themselves at home on the back steps, where they poo and trip everyone up when they are not chewing everyone's shoes. The ones who came to us in matched pairs also set vigorously about duplicating themselves.

Most significantly, once they become boring (and this can sometimes take days, sometimes hours) there seems to be one focal person who, for reasons inexplicable, becomes responsible for feeding the whole hippy commune — Mother. As if she didn't have enough to do already!

Somewhere along the line, matters have to be taken into hand.

The ducklings, Sweetie Pie and Mighty Duck, became a nightmare of aggressive hissing, then grew into gluttonous converters of perfectly good food, leaving a chequerboard of squishy duck droppings on the back steps. They were converted to Sunday dinner. The kids fussed, but well, that's life! Such matters are part of normal omnivorous behaviour, with a special twist to bypass the middleman. It was a "commercial decision".

However, there was no pretence about the piglets. While they were undoubtedly cute to start with, they only ever had one purpose. They had a great lifestyle at our place. They quickly outgrew their pens and became, to our dismay, huge free-ranging adult pigs. They made themselves thoroughly at home, wallowing in any available mud and entering any open doors, usually in that order.

Finally, when I made the harrowing discovery that they had systematically dismantled my garden, and eaten my agapanthus clump plus vast quantities of lawn, they were declared Pork and Bacon, respectively and forthwith.

The kids struggled to digest this apparently dreadful travesty. Although they happily digested the pork and bacon.

We adults believe the table is a rightful destination for a pig. Jock finds it rather shocking, hence his insecurity about how fond of the cat he should become.

The cat is safe from our table. Life and death, however, are just part of the daily struggle.

TWENTY-THREE

Fairy Interesting

We are into fairies in a big way at our place.

And we are really lucky because it just so happens that we have fairies living in our garden. This is an amazing coincidence, and five-year-old Lou is rapt.

Believe me, we are not allowed to take our luck for granted. It permeates our lives.

We communicate with our fairies—it's a pretty heavy relationship. We converse with them. We confide our innermost secrets and family shortcomings in them. We leave gifts out for them, draw pictures for them, build them paddling ponds in hot weather, and worry about them when it is cold. Within (perceived) earshot we live our lives, on a verbal level at least, in a way that we feel would most please them. We ask them for things and sometimes, if we are young enough, they actually give them to us.

It's a hot topic at our place, and very satisfying.

I say "we" in a purely de-facto sense here. The family is

ably represented by Louisa on the fairy front. Most of us hardly take much notice of them at all, except to mind our language in the garden. Lou is the family's self-appointed fairy public relations officer.

Her main operational thrust is communication. Regular letter writing. Which becomes a bit of a drag, if you can just picture it, because this is where mother becomes indispensible on yet another front.

Lou is only a beginner at writing. Really, really small writing is beyond her. So it falls to me to act as her scribe.

Also, as it happens, I get the scribe's job from the other angle as well because, although our fairies are smart, they have not had the benefit of education. They can't write their own letters in reply.

I tolerate this. It's purely a matter of a lack of opportunity in our garden. There is no literacy snobbery in this mother's heart, and that is why she feels it is unnecessary for Lou to know who exactly does the writing of the tiny letters from a fairy called Winterbelle which she finds rolled up in the eremophila bush outside our window. The actual authorship is just a matter of semantics. It gives her so much pleasure, this little middle child who needs someone in the world to single her out and make her feel special. Who am I to disillusion her about her fairies?

The letter writing and stuff, the good behaviour and polite talk in the garden—those are the upside of having fairies in your garden. But there is a downside too.

We are now obliged to redesign our garden according to our fairies' perceived tastes. We must weed, maintain and water our garden only if and when it suits their needs.

We must plant seedlings that bear flowers that make good fairy homes. We must not disturb particularly weed-infested patches of garden for fear of ripping apart Winterbelle's life in some way. It would be better if we didn't water at all, not ever.

There are a few conflicts of interest between a small child intent on preserving a living commune (including an orphan fairy godchild she herself has named, at the fairies' request, Raindrop) and a boring, unholy adult whose major interest in the garden is getting it thoroughly wet, pruning according to her own desire, pulling out weeds and fertilising with horse poo.

Fairies don't like horse poo tipped on them.

So, all you pragmatists out there, is this a lesson on how telling tales can get out of hand? Or is it an exercise in giving unparalleled pleasure to a little girl who is learning about commitment, how to nurture, imagine, cherish, conduct friendships, give, take, dream and love?

TWENTY-FOUR

Life's a Bummer at the Tail End

When you are lowest in the rank and file of a family, you end up with a particular outlook on life. Only when you've been there can you relate to others of the same caste. I've been there; I can relate to it. And from the perspective of more years than I care to admit, I can assure you that it is a legacy which is nigh impossible to shake off. My older sisters still boss me around.

I was the youngest in my family till I was usurped ignominiously at the age of ten. Being youngest had lots going for it, like that the older ones had broken my parents in pretty well. By the time I came along, I could get away with blue murder.

Worn down by years of parenting, oldies are just too exhausted to argue effectively when your list of social engagements at the coast at age 14 resembles a week in the life of Madonna in her heyday. Besides, they had seen my three older sisters survive.

Those three paved the way for every major life-changing event that traditionally happens in a child's life, and took the edge off the mystery and terror of the totally unknown.

There's also the benefit that you learn the vernacular of your older siblings' peers in the comfort of your own home. So you don't have to wait until you are enrolled at school to get onto the latest cool words you think your parents don't know, use or (gross thought!) actually do.

But there are downsides too; being dressed in cast-off clothes is a big one. Being called spoilt by your siblings is another. And being the baby is only of benefit in some circumstances, not many of which are appreciated by your siblings.

Then when you are suddenly no longer the baby! But that is another story.

As a tail-ender, you seem to spend your life fighting to be taken seriously long after the ties of family of origin are nothing more than frayed, disused apron strings.

But every family has to have its youngest. My family of origin had me for 10 years, and my own family has Jock. And let me tell you, Jock will not be usurped.

I am aware that an emotive era is rolling up behind Jock. I can give him my full attention because I'm not exhausted by pregnancy or taken up with the needs of a younger child. While I love them all with equal passion, somehow it happens that I can notice more about this tail-ender kid, this combination of Lou and Sam whom he imitates with the osmotic expertise of infancy.

It's not just the psychological effect of being smallest that makes a youngest evolve in a particular way. It's the perspective from which you get to view the world. It puts a unique slant on your handle on things.

The other day, we were visiting Robbie and Bodo, friends who live in the Esk Valley. We stood about for a while, admiring their beautiful Princess Alexandria parrot, Puff.

Puff flew from shoulder to shoulder, flaunting his plumage, chirping tunefully and being generally cute, basking in the glory of our undivided attention. We all thought he was the most enchanting pet we had ever seen.

"Look at his tail feathers!" exclaimed one of us bigger people, who had a good view of proceedings. "Look at his crest!" said another.

Jock, age two, underfoot, unnoticed, knee high to a grasshopper, but eloquent as ever and not to be outdone with complimentary comments, exhorted, "Look at *he's* bum!"

Well, I guess he just sees things from a different angle to the rest of us. Literally.

TWENTY-FIVE

Veronica

My friend Roni didn't make it to our birthday, Rob's and mine. She slipped away a week early, leaving us who loved her quietly bereft.

It was her time. She was old and ill, her body worn out while her mind was still intact. What better time to go? In the end, she didn't suffer the ignominy of losing her mind as well as the strength of her once-powerful body.

We knew this, so it took the edge off our sadness. But still we felt dreadfully the core pain of our loss.

Many people who lead magnificent lives don't make it into the news, either in life or in dying. So it was with Roni. While we deal with our grief and get on with our lives just as she would want, that seems somehow to belie the fact that this person led an extraordinary life, and was an inspiration to many people. The world should know that she left a more powerful mark than most average souls, and that she lives on in many of us who admired her because she was an extraordinary woman.

Roni lived through times that younger generations can only try to imagine. Born with the proverbial silver spoon in her mouth, her destiny was to lead a privileged life. She was part of the old squattocracy, educated at an exclusive boarding school, and taught the genteel skills of a society lady.

In the 1930s, she was sent to London to make her society debut. Presented at Court to the King, that brazen, flame-haired colonial beauty defied convention and looked the old boy in the eye—a shockingly bold breach of protocol, and a trademark of her character.

But Destiny will not be taken for granted. The world was turned upside down soon after, and an era became forever bygone. First the Depression, when hunger and honest desperation roamed the roads, touching everyone. Although cushioned from the worst effects of those times, the social elite saw other possibilities, a darker side of life. The war that followed hard on its heels was darker still. It brought loss and hardship, without discrimination or recognition of social barriers.

In fact, it changed things forever.

Roni the society girl nursed the wounded soldiers from the Pacific War, and later the shells of men who returned from the Asian POW camps. It was tough, and she saw some dreadful things. Cold comfort in the fact that an entire generation was dragged, one way or another, into the same horrific events. The characters of this generation were forged in a crucible of fire. They were all destined to value life according to what they had seen.

Roni brought to the motherhood of four fine sons and tribes of their friends the strength of her survival of those times. Life went on to throw the book at her. She took it up, read it, and laughed. Times of privilege long gone, she survived the storms of bankruptcy, the loss of her possessions in a cyclone, and a near-fatal car accident, throwing her considerable weight into enriching any community in which she lived. She helped provide for her family in times which were always difficult, but what was extraordinary about her was that she never complained; life was always an adventure. The gusto with which she approached both the simple and complex things in her life and, eventually, her death, drew people to her for strength and inspiration.

She was always either strapped for cash or high on the hog, always occupied with some new venture—plaiting, weaving, watercolour landscape painting, brilliantly sketching horses, embroidering, gardening, studying with U3A, photography, fabric painting, playing cards or travelling. Just having life was wealth to her, who had seen so much death, and we could all take a leaf from her book.

You went to her for a shoulder to lean on and, despite or because of the heavy hand she had so often been dealt, to be reminded of the lighter side of life, and the unimportance of so much trivia with which we burden ourselves.

In the end, breathless and suffering, with her beloved sons around her, she laughed in the face of Death. She cocked her snoot at that old Tyrant and went out as she had lived—defiant, job done, no regrets.

―

Veronica Cox Chilcott was a family friend. She and my dad and their immediate families were friends from the time of their early childhood on the Darling Downs. Later, by coincidence, she and my mum shared digs in Townsville during World War II, and became lifelong friends. Roni's fourth son, Rob, and I, my parents' fourth daughter, were the "twins", born within hours of each other at the Southport Hospital in Queensland.

TWENTY-SIX

A Mother's Job

I have let it be known without a hint of subtlety that anyone in our house who leaves a bunch of red cotoneaster berries in their shorts pocket EVER AGAIN will be made very short work of by their mother.

What a disaster on washing day, as I discovered to my horror. As well as finding the berries and their gizzards stuck to everything in the washing machine at the end of the final rinse, another pocketful escaped in the dryer and got all over what they missed in the wash.

In response, when I stated my case severely, I was told in no uncertain terms that it is a mother's job to empty everyone's pockets before loading the washing machine.

Ha! A mother's job, is it? I'll give you a mother's job!

A mother's job, like a pocketful of cotoneaster berries in the wash, is a permanent commitment. It can be as simple as washing one person's sheets every morning, knowing that those same sheets will be right back in the wash next morning.

Or it can be as complex as taking the time to put her kids in the way of every opportunity within range. That involves Mum's Taxi. And that's when you know you're alive.

In addition to the basics of family living, you find yourself on a frenetic roundabout of extra-curricular activities. You become besotted by the irrational belief that if you slacken your pace, you are falling short in the jostle for your kid's lifestyle completeness.

Yep, I came right in, spinner. Once, I compared notes with a Brisbane friend, expressing some scorn about the way we all seemed to haul our kids off to every imaginable activity to the extent that they had no time just to sit in a patch of dust and be kids. Much as I used to. And look how I turned out!

My friend agreed with me that it was out of hand. "We keep our little Billy to a minimum; after all, he's only in Year One. He just does swimming on Mondays and Thursdays, violin on Wednesdays, karate on Fridays, extra maths on Tuesdays and soccer on Saturdays. We don't agree with all that extra stuff. We think it's totally exhausting for them."

I went fairly quiet after that. And somehow, time and experience have glossed over my strong opinions on the subject. I am now aware that there is such a smorgasbord of wonderful, exciting things for kids to become involved in nowadays that I only wish I could have another go at being a child.

But for the time being I am a mother, and my job description has taken a sudden and shocking leap into another dimension. Forget Mum's Taxi! That is but a small part of the job. This year alone my maternal CV has blown out with enough new qualifications to fill my hard drive.

In the name of commitment to one of my daughter's clubs, I currently have 20 packets of biscuits to sell to my already wary friends at two bucks apiece. In my back pocket, I have a book of raffle tickets from my older son's club to sell to them once they have their wallets out for the biscuits.

I have made a promise, which I intend to keep, to stand at a street stall on my day off work and sell more raffle tickets to the unsuspecting public, and then to rush to a secret destination in support of my daughter's club and help make approximately 3000 lamingtons which I will then tout around my own neighbourhood, and my friends if they don't see me coming first.

I have already sold 35 packets of freesia bulbs from a Kindy fundraising catalogue. Another fundraiser for Jock involved scrubbing and dressing up the whole family and dragging them, protesting loudly, to a makeshift photographic studio for a family portrait. Then I bought about 20 more photographs than I actually needed, and paid for them through the nose, because I was given only five minutes to decide which ones I wanted and said, like everyone else in the queue, "Oh, I'll just take the lot, thanks," as I rushed off to our next family appointment. That was before I realised Lou's tattoos from the church fete had not been removed, and were the outstanding feature of the expensive photograph package.

I have gardened at Kindy in my smart work clothes to avoid roster duty washing the Kindy curtains. I have sat in the drizzling rain for one and a half hours guarding backpacks belonging to 25 cub scouts while they trekked to the bottom of a waterfall. I have sat wrapped up in a blanket under the stars on a freezing night, too far away from the bonfire to benefit from any of the warmth we were promised in the notice, watching Gumnut Guides do their nocturnal "thing".

We are currently finding sponsors for a skipathon; oh yes, and sponsors also for a readathon, with two participants. We earmark potential sponsors for when we next need sponsors for something.

Not to mention soccer—soccer for him, soccer for her. Two different practice times a week, and two separate match times on a Saturday. I sit with other mothers on the sidelines, drinking coffee and feeding lollipops to my four-year-old, thinking, "Yay! This is what I dreamed about."

And it is. I'm a bloody wonderful mother. But I still shout at the kids, and their white sports shirts are nonetheless stained with cotoneaster berry juice. How IS that?

TWENTY-SEVEN

My Perfect Boy

Parenthood is not for the faint-hearted. Nor the idealistic, or the dull-witted, or the slow-to-start-in-the-mornings.

No doubt that is why God thought up the idea of having two parents, so one can fill in when the other's biorhythms are sluggish. Thank you, God, for not making me an amoeba.

Faint-hearted I may be at times, but not having read the job description, I nonetheless became a mother. It was different for me because I KNEW that *my* children, unlike all those others you hear about, would be absolutely perfect. My maternal instinct, tempered with a little idealism and booted along no doubt by a dull wit, told me this.

Which is why the events that unfolded one time in our household came as such a terrible shock to me.

I was tearfully informed that those who know about these things know that running shoes are much more comfortable to wear to school than leather lace-ups. Plus, they are much trendier.

I was told that (for reasons the teller could not explain) the laces on running shoes do not come undone as easily as those on leather school shoes.

And I was assured that for these and other highly practical and essential reasons, which included playing soccer at lunchtime, my eldest son must really, really have a pair of black running shoes instead of his (new) leather school shoes to wear to school.

And soon. In fact (sensing in my look the likelihood of success within his grasp) that very day.

Yes, I have always been a fairly soft touch. I was impressed with the practicality of the reasons delivered with such passion, and convinced that Sam's life at school would improve if he were to have more comfy shoes. So I tentatively agreed.

The child's father, however, was unimpressed.

At breakfast, the edict went up, not to be ignored. "There will be no black running shoes bought until the black leather ones are worn out." There was no arguing with the sense, practicality and finality of that. We bowed to the pressure, I with my head hung in shame at even contemplating such excess.

Then a strange thing happened. Although almost every day during the total chaos of our morning preparations we have last-minute frantic hunts for missing shoes, hats, lunch boxes and other vital paraphernalia, these are inevitably found, albeit in all kinds of strange places.

This day, however, the black leather shoes were not to be found anywhere.

Everyone joined in the hunt, which went high and low, inside and outside. But they were nowhere.

Poor Sam had absolutely no recollection of where he had taken them off.

The poor kid had to wear his white running shoes to school, and take a note for the teacher.

The father said, "I bet the sneaky little bugger's hidden them!" and the mother replied, with passion, "What, your son—my son? Sneaky? He's only six! Anyway, he wouldn't be that smart. Absolutely no way, no way at all."

It was really looking as if we would have to get him a new pair of shoes.

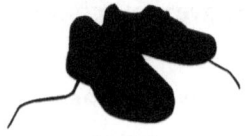

At lunchtime, I asked a friend who had been visiting the evening before, "Did you happen to see Sam's shoes when you collected your son from our place yesterday?"

"Yes," she said. "They were right there on the living room floor."

I told her the circumstances of their mysterious disappearance and she threw back her head and laughed heartily. I was pretty annoyed. She obviously did not know that my child, if for no other reason than purely on the basis of nobility via genetics, was not capable of a devious act.

But just on spec, that evening we announced that there would be no black running shoes bought until the leather shoes were found; and that in the meantime, only slippers were to be worn to school instead.

The black leather shoes were found within nanoseconds. They had somehow fallen down the back of a cupboard.

Strange, that.

TWENTY-EIGHT

Strangers in the Night

There was a bit of a fuss at our place one morning when we still had a baby in the house. Something was found under the bed. This cast an uncomfortable shadow of doubt over my credibility as a capable housekeeper and a responsible mother.

Although time and kilos had wrought havoc with both our ample forms, the Old Boy and I shared a regular-sized marital bed in those halcyon days.

In addition to this, the Old Boy seemed to have always felt the need to accommodate an invisible person on his side, near the edge. Or perhaps it was simply a contingency measure in case some poor homeless person should arrive unannounced during the night and need sleeping room.

Whatever, there is always enough room for another person on the Old Boy's other side.

Then there is me in the leftover space, of which there is not very much, while there is quite a lot of me.

And intermittently throughout the night, for quite a number of years, at least one kid, including whoever was the current baby.

To overcome the problem of my falling out of bed due to lack of space, the baby's cot was wedged up against my side of the bed. This had double value, because when the baby woke up for a feed I didn't even need to open my eyes. I just reached over in the dark and hauled him/her out of his/her cot without fear of dropping him/her in any intervening space.

It was a well thought-out plan, and awfully convenient, even if I do say so myself.

After a few kids, you have most of the time and motion exercises essential to motherhood down to a fine art. So expert was I, that I could even change the baby's nappy on my knee in the pitch dark without getting out of bed, and with my eyes closed if necessary. This was usually around 2.30am, not a good time for vibrant awareness.

This practice also served as a valuable survival tool, and I recommend it to young mothers. It means that neither party involved wakes fully, thus minimising lost sleep.

This particular morning, however, we struck a hitch. The Old Boy has an innate abhorrence (not uncommon in men) of normal bodily functions, especially around babies—he always made a dramatic display of gagging at dirty nappies. We all knew that this was so that no one would ever expect him to handle them, and it worked, since it brooked no argument.

In addition, he had an abnormally well-developed sense of smell. His sniffer-dog's nose for unusual smells led him on this fateful day to bend down double in uncharacteristic manner and discover under the bed the source of a familiar unmentionable odour.

The thing he found had fallen there of its own accord during my nocturnal nappy-change. Its discovery somewhat upset our united attitude towards my night-time routine, which to date had not been tested for its now obvious need to accommodate the elementary contingency: "What if the nappy discarded in the dark is not such a simple one?" And following on from that, "What if its contents are inadvertently dislodged?"

My first impulse, when I was hauled down to the bedroom with dramatic suspense and animated gestures to inspect what he had found, was to blurt out, "Wow, lucky that didn't end up in the bed with us!"

However, the Old Boy did not see it that way. He and the invisible person might have been grossly offended. They might have been inconvenienced at a dreadfully early hour. In a rather unforgettable way. So, I was made to realise, might I. Possibly by default.

The way I see it, you can't please everyone. And for a working mother, sleep is survival, and survival is paramount!

TWENTY-NINE

Looking for Me

If these pages were the stuff of romantic fiction, I would tell you that I have spent the afternoon pacing the floor, wondering what to do with myself and waiting for 6pm and the cheap phone rate so I could make the long-distance call to check on the status of Gran, her darling baby (my husband) and our mutual kids.

I would probably add that I was genuinely surprised to be afflicted thus, since I had looked forward to this time so eagerly. And I would say that I had honestly thought I would relax and enjoy myself when they went away for a few days but alas, it seemed that the emptiness of the situation was too much for my maternal breast to bear. That my brief respite was ruined by longing and concern for my family.

However, while poetic licence is an essential stock in my trade, fiction is not my brief. And I am here to tell you that I have had a delightful afternoon unfettered by obligations and time constraints, other than those dictated by the setting of the sun, and—this is the real luxury—alone.

I finished work early and sauntered into a coffee lounge, where I relaxed with a book entitled *Amazing Phenomena*, thoughtfully provided by the management for people with time on their hands.

So there I sat, with time on my hands. Languorously I sipped my coffee and flipped through the entire book, ingesting marvellously useless data. Did you know, for example, that Elvis Presley is in fact still alive and possibly living in your neighbourhood? Or that Marilyn Monroe was probably murdered by the CIA?

Gosh!

People rushed in and out, slaves to their various schedules, yet I sat, a free woman, while the inside details of the capture of the Yorkshire Ripper were graphically revealed to me.

Sated, I yawned and brought myself back to my surroundings. The dregs of my coffee were cold. I was actually still sitting there with an empty cup in front of me!

This is very satisfactory, thought I. Very relaxing.

Such was the intensity of my appreciation of that state that a woman at the next table nervously reached for her handbag when I walked past her. She must have thought I was high on some drug. And indeed, I was. The drug of freedom.

I came home to an empty house where only my own mess greeted me. I put on my joggers and went for a walk up the mountain, alone and unencumbered. There was a dog at my heels, but no small person clinging to my back or trailing along behind wailing, "Mu-um! Wait for me! Marm!

I've got a prickle, help me! Mum, is it 5.30? Can we go back now and watch *The Simpsons*?"

Home again, I sat alone on the garden seat amid the chaos that was once my garden, relishing my solitary repast of wine and olives. This is thoroughly satisfactory, I thought to myself, and had some more.

I cooked nothing for dinner because nothing was what I wanted. And there was no-one who might have wanted more or who expected me to prepare it.

Lord, please don't think I am ungrateful for the four lavish blessings you have bestowed on me over the past 10 years. Please don't think I don't cherish every precious moment (well, almost) while my babies are so very dependent on me.

I listen when my contemporaries whose young have flown the nest say wistfully that it will be over all too soon. I listen and I believe them.

Still, I am in it, and have been steeped in it for 10 years now. During that time, someone called Me has been hounded out of my life by demands and hangers on. I miss her and cherish this small time to seek her out.

I am going to squeeze every moment out of these three nights and four precious days, a sunny island in an ocean of commitment.

I am going to commune with this Me and see if there's anything left I recognise. I'm going to do it in silence and solitude insofar as I am able, and I am going to relish it.

So far, so good.

THIRTY

All That Remains

Beautiful blonde bob framing a rosebud face. Flashing come-hither-and-do-as-I-say-this-very-minute green eyes. Uppity little nose, seductive scarlet lips curled around a mouth full of baby teeth. Chubby little hands perched on perky little hips, all balanced on sturdy little legs that are set to be shapelier than her mother's.

The best little girl in all the world is about to turn five.

Winter's chrysanthemums are perfect after a little rain. The geraniums are flourishing; even the daisies are putting on a decent show. What better combination of excuses to have a garden party?

Fairy invitations are prepared and sent to more people than originally envisaged.

No effort is to be spared for this most blessed of occasions—a yearly ritual it has become. Every May. The Birthday Party.

Mother digs out the high school cookbook. The section

on deportment is a right treat: "*A lady walks putting toe down first, then the heel, holding gloves with fingers outwards while they are not being worn.*" How I remember practising this rather ridiculous exercise in incoordination to the shrieking mirth of my amazed and ever-to-be-ladyless family. Now, despite the passage of the years, the book still has the best recipe for cupcakes ever invented.

The cakes are cooked in batches of three dozen at a time and, along with the kitchen bench, are iced in a kaleidoscope of colours with the expert help of small hands. The longed-for chocolate cake with Smarties on top is ordered from the bakery—Mum never was a reliable cooker of larger cakes.

The Old Boy cranks up the protesting mower, idle through years of drought. He spreads the clippings artfully on the garden, cleverly concealing the weeds. Then he whipper-snips the garden edges to within centimetres of their lives.

Wow! It looks like Paradise; yep, I could live here myself!

I deliver the annual instructions about how to play host: don't ask where the present is; don't even *expect* a present! Be kind to everyone, make sure everyone has a good time. No chasing the chooks; no climbing on to the roof; no kids inside, especially if it has rained.

Then the occasion and the guests arrive. Everyone is so delirious with excitement that all instructions, agreements and promises fly straight out the window.

The chooks have a helluva day, and go off the lay for weeks. The dogs pig out on cupcakes. The kids can't find a ladder so the roof stays empty. The chrysanthemums lose their heads, and the weeds slowly emerge from under the grass clippings, which turn out to be great snowball substitutes.

One child spends the entire party, unnoticed, honing his landscaping skills on my new drystone wall—my pride and joy, just out of sight around the corner of the house. He dismantles it completely. Every now and then he rushes up to his mum and says, "Nearly finished, Mummy, just got a bit to go!" and disappears off again with an air of great purpose, while all the other mums fondly, and completely unawares, congratulate her on his adorable industry.

The parents stand about, sipping coffee and champagne in the warm winter sun. It's rather a lovely way to spend the afternoon.

There are kids hanging from every branch. Boys chase girls (not that they like them); girls chase boys.

What do they do with them when they catch them?

Why, they keep them hostage, then let them go then catch them again, until a better idea comes along.

Cupcakes are scoffed hand over fist. I intercept one kid, whose mother does not allow him to eat sugar, heading out the back door with at least a dozen cakes stuffed down his shirt. He later vomits on the front steps.

The bowl of fruit that was prepared with such sanctimonious intent to impress the no-sugar mother is completely ignored. The lawn, and a few stray toddlers, get thoroughly watered during the obligatory cordial fight. The day is pronounced perfect, no stone unturned (except my as-yet-undiscovered former drystone wall) to make it a success.

Sitting in the debris of a seemingly perfect day, we ask the tired birthday girl how she enjoyed her party.

"It was really great, thanks. But ..." and to our surprise, she bursts into tragic sobs. A dreadful misdemeanour is revealed through hiccups of misery. "But I wish Nicholas hadn't brought his baby sister."

"Why not? She's only a baby! What on earth did she do?"

(Sob) "She ate the only pink Smartie on my birthday cake!"

Oh shame, Nicholas's baby sister. Shame.

THIRTY-ONE

Bad Dog Month

It has been a bad dog month. Definitely, a bad dog month. It is a strange phenomenon—have kids, have pets. As if the rearing of children and all it entails is not enough, some of us feel that a family is not complete without an avian, canine or feline component. Or perhaps all three.

We belong to the "all three, and more" category of family. But this story is about the canine family members. Although I could speculate on cannibalism in the aviary (a strange series of disappearances and one fat lovebird remaining). Or that the cat recently had kittens who think the loo is under the piano.

But I won't.

As life will have it, a month or so ago we were cruising along, thinking our family was complete. We were doing just fine as a two-dog family, and all was well in the Garden of Eden. Then in the blink of an eye, we became a one-dog family.

So the children and I ameliorated our grief by spending long hours discussing the type of dog we would get to replace our deceased red kelpie, Missy. We would get something different this time. But would it be a Jack Russell terrier, or a cocker spaniel, or a golden retriever? Or perhaps a little poodle—but would we let it into the house?

Would we get a boy dog or a girl dog?

We dreamed on and on, till we started to feel better about the loss of Missy. Having so many different breeds to choose from was a great comfort.

The same could not be said for replacing a mother, as I very subtly pointed out each time the subject came up. Just a little public relations exercise. Such genuine opportunities for promoting a personal cause do not arise often.

But there was a major hitch in our plans for choosing a new dog. We did not account for the independence of grown men. We arrived home one day—and there was our new dog. Just like that. No prior consultation or consensus or any of those modern, gimmicky, family-bonding concepts that are supposed to be the opiate of today's masses. The Old Boy came home from the world-famous Warwick Pig & Calf Sale with a kelpie pup, a girl with very sharp teeth—and that was the end of that.

Or so we thought.

Our individual disappointments were politely put aside and nature took its course. The pup was round and red and altogether adorable. The kids called her Lady, and we all loved and cherished her as a new family member. She still smelt of that delicious puppy smell, and got up to all that charming puppy mischief with our shoes at the back door.

You'd find the inevitable little puppy messages strewn all over the back patio, and the odd one smuggled itself into the house on the bottom of our shoes. All in all, it was just that extra straw on the camel's back a working mother needed, because naturally enough, once the pup arrived she mysteriously became Mum's responsibility, the way these things happen.

Don't you just know all about that one?

Within a day or two, we realised that it was a very risky business venturing outside the back door. Lady, energetically chewing Missy's former spot on the coir mat, no sooner saw your foot appear than she would latch on. Nor was it easy, or even advisable to prise her off, because a prised-off and underfoot Lady was far more dangerous to your health than razor-sharp teeth, or the odd bit of dog poo.

We humans worked out ingenious ways of surviving the terror, such as using other doors or staying inside. We also had enough innate intelligence, if not patience, to understand that this was but a phase in the life of a family dog. This too would pass, we philosophised.

But old Hero, the blue heeler, had none of these qualities. The situation was too much for his age, stage and grouchy disposition.

For a week or so, he suffered stoically. Then one night, under intense provocation, he cracked.

Just what portion of his anatomy the pup latched onto when Hero sat down does not bear thinking about. But latch on she did, and herein lies this sad tale.

From the laundry, I heard a cheeky puppy bark, followed by a growl, followed by a loud and sickening crunch, followed by an ominously brief yelp, followed by an awful silence. And oh my! Sadness, sadness and more sadness.

A swift and nervous inspection of the coir mat showed us the picture, and it was not pretty. Lady lay rigid. Thoroughly chastised, she struggled on with brain damage for weeks. It was a long and torturous journey and in the end, she lost the battle.

It was a bad dog month, that one.

Personally, I don't remember even wanting a dog in the very beginning.

THIRTY-TWO

Cries of Snakebite

There are people who think it's weird to keep plants as pets—which is sort of what gardening is, when you think about it.

I am not one of those people. I love my pet plants, and I get amongst 'em as often as I can.

My neighbour, Gai, said gardens harboured vermin, and provided a safe haven for snakes. I thought she was a tragic, quite frankly.

"If a snake can't hear me huffing and puffing around in my own garden, and get out of my way, then it's deaf—or dead," I boldly retorted. "Gardening is too good for my soul to be worried about small things like SNAKES. Give us a break!"

I even snickered a little. I tried to imagine anyone's being pathetic enough to eschew keeping a garden just because of the wild possibility of running into a snake.

Oh, for goodness sakes!

Well, there came a time when I went very quiet on the subject, and it was not so long after Gai and I had had our animated discussion on the subject.

Not to put too fine a point on it, I stood on a brown snake in my own garden. Just like that. Snakes must be bloody deaf after all. Well, this one certainly wasn't dead.

You don't stand on a snake on purpose. Snakes don't go about waiting to be stood on. We just coincided, rather dramatically, and recoiled simultaneously, but not before the snake had a go at me.

It was a simple meeting, and a day like any other day. There I was, reaching up to the patio for a fitting for the garden hose, when I felt something wriggling under my foot. I looked down just in time to see a brown snake strike at my trousered leg. Immediately realising it had made a big boo-boo, it beat a hasty and horrified retreat.

Ere my life passed before my eyes, Gai's words zoomed across the screen of my vision like a subliminal TV ad.

Then I remembered that when I was small, Dad got bitten by a brown snake. So I realised at once that there was a precedent; it was indeed possible that it could happen to someone in *my* family. Even me!

When Dad copped it, I was morbidly impressed by the fact that he did not at first realise he had been bitten. He had jumped down off the grain harvester when, in mid-flight, he saw that he had caught a brown snake by the tail in the tines of the header comb.

The snake was raised up in a rage, ready to get its fangs into something in revenge. Dad unaccountably lost his normal powers of instant reversal when in mid-fall, so he was It.

He landed, was struck at, but felt nothing, and continued what he was doing. Suddenly he was overcome by the venom, and realised his mistake. It was only by sheer willpower that he managed to drag himself home to get help, by which time it was almost too late.

After a frantic dash to town, he survived but he was very ill for ages. Now as I stood there watching my snake's tail disappear under the house, the maudlin details of Dad's mishap came back to me in minute detail.

Here I was, a mother of three young babes who still needed me, and I had been struck at in my turn! I waited a minute or two, but could not decide whether my pounding heart was a symptom or a result.

Panicking, and with visions of my babies as orphans flashing through my now-feverish brain, I rushed inside to consult the St John First Aid Manual.

"The victim's heart will be palpitating", it said. Palpitating? My heart was leaping out of my chest with sheer terror. Oh God! It got me! I panicked, whereupon my heart nearly stopped altogether.

"*There will be two small puncture marks where the fangs entered the victim's flesh.*" With trembling hands I peeled off my jeans and sure enough, there were two spots that *could* have been puncture marks. Well, sort of, not quite the same size or where the snake had struck at me but since by now my whole leg was also palpitating, it was hard to tell.

Waiting for confirmation that the venom was taking effect was like waiting for the next contraction at the onset of childbirth. Was that one or wasn't it? Should we go now or shouldn't we? I had oscillated like this before Louisa's birth until, like my father before me, it was only by sheer effort of will that I kept that baby from being born in Silver, the old Holden, being driven at 160 kilometres per hour by a grim-faced, half-shaved, soon-to-be-father of two.

That same father, unimpressed by the lack of palpable symptoms after half an hour or so, was seriously unsympathetic of my "snakebite". It was only when (at my own insistence) he took me to the hospital where some medico stuck a needle into it that I got some real tongue-clicking sympathy. Indeed, it could have been nasty. It could have been one of the kids. I could have been wearing shorts. It could, in fact, have bitten me.

But it hadn't.

And what, may well you ask, did Gai have to say about this episode? You surely don't think she heard about it, do you? Not from me, anyway.

THIRTY-THREE

Intimate Family Confessions

My children have fleas. We all do.

It's because we have a cat.

It's a family commitment, having the cat, one that we made because we were involuntarily harbouring mice; lots and lots of mice. That made it easier for our kids to persuade us that our lives would be greatly improved with a household cat to love, cherish and obey.

The theory was that it would also kill the mice.

Perhaps flustered by the mice, and ever hopeful, we did not think through the full ramifications of cat ownership. It was only after we were thoroughly committed to the cat that we discovered the odd downside. Minor things, really—flea plagues which lead to flea bites which lead to flea bombs.

And my mother won't come and stay with us because of the fleas.

Being crafty little buggers, the fleas waited until we had

all become quite fond of the cat. To be fair to the cat, it did, during its nine months with us actually catch at least two mice—one feral, one not-so-feral.

The not-so-feral one was one of a pair of domestic mice bought at great expense from the pet shop.

Considering how we have been persecuted by plague mice over the years, I find it hard to believe that we ever agreed to this futile exercise in pet ownership. How on earth my children managed to persuade me to let them keep domestic mice, I do not know.

At any rate, they wore me down and the pet mice became temporary members of the family. The idea was that they would be safely incarcerated, while the thousands of feral mice would roam blithely around the house, creating havoc, but mostly being ignored by the cat.

The cat entered into the spirit of family commitment immediately the pet mice arrived home from the pet shop. Within minutes, to the sound of the frantic wails of small children, she ate the black one with relish. (This is, of course, just a manner of speaking. The cat is spoiled but we do not serve relish with its meals.)

That was one instance of proof that the cat had actually eaten a mouse. For some reason, the kids saw it differently and wailed bitterly for a replacement.

Yes, of course there was a replacement. And quickly.

Now, a word of advice for anyone considering succumbing to childish exhortations for a pet mouse: the smell of pet mice creates much the same ambience as that of feral mice.

My mother won't come and stay with us because of the ambience of the mice.

The other confirmed mouse kill was when, with truly feline panache, the cat strutted into the kitchen during breakfast, meowing through her nose because her mouth was full of a bemused and tortured mouse. Having ensured that she had the full attention of her captive audience, she proceeded to delicately dismember the struggling little rodent before our outraged eyes, savouring each tiny morsel—disgustingly and sensually—and eyeing us with a look that said, "Go on, say something. Defy nature. I am but a cat, after all, and this is my job."

From time to time we also have lice—bird lice. This makes an interesting alternative to the occasional urgent wrangle with common old nits, which naturally involve the entire family and are part and parcel of the experience of childhood. And those closely associated with it.

Bird lice are but a temporary ailment and easily avoided. The best thing about them is how we come to acquire them. It involves a very jolly trip to the Queen Mary Falls at nearby Killarney and a refreshing bushwalk—and possibly an ice cream too if we have all behaved ourselves—before feeding the native parrots that flock to the kiosk at sunset to chance their luck. They sit on every horizontal surface the human body offers, and daintily peck seed from eagerly outstretched hands. When they are truly relaxed on your head, they nonchalantly, and probably with no intended malice, part with their lice.

It's not until you get home that you become aware of their magnanimous gesture.

My mother doesn't know about the bird lice and, quite frankly, we don't see why she needs to know.

THIRTY-FOUR

The Animal Advocate

There are many rewards for living long enough to get "older".

For one thing, your past comes back to meet you.

If you have lived long enough to accumulate a reasonable amount of past you have probably gained the wisdom to avoid the bits you don't want to repeat. A bit like crossing the street to escape an unwanted encounter in the present.

There is, after all, both good and bad about your past coming back to you. As you reap rewards, so you also pay dues. I paid my dues, long afterwards, for not becoming a committed vegan/animal liberationist when I had the opportunity to sign up for life many years ago.

One of the more esoteric organisations I worked for during the creation of my past was the Scottish Society for the Prevention of Vivisection. This gloriously named organisation had its headquarters in Edinburgh. I played a very minor role in its success, and am pleased to note that it has since, and not before time, changed its name to Advocates for Animals.

The Society's basic philosophy was admirable. I quite agree that it is horrible to use animals for scientific experiments. Especially when it's only in the production of some cosmetics; what justification, for human vanity?

Though I felt strongly about these matters, I never became strident about it. I never wore plastic shoes rather than leather. I like a doona with real down and a pillow with real feathers.

I enjoy a good juicy steak, and even when I was working for the Scottish Society for the Prevention of Vivisection, bless its Gaelic heart, I regularly ate haggis.

Well, haggis was as close to real meat as my British working holiday budget would allow.

Not to mention jelly. I LOVE jelly! Know what gelatine's made of? Don't find out.

My passive life membership of the Scottish Society for the Prevention of Vivisection was not sufficient dedication to the cause of animal advocacy for Lou at the age of six.

I was working away in the kitchen one day when she rushed in breathlessly and urgently asked for a spoon. Knowing I shouldn't, but as it eventuated, glad I did, I asked her what it was for.

"There's a fly stuck in the toilet," she sobbed, weeping and trembling. "It's going to drown, Mummy. I have to help it get out!" Her humane concern might have touched even my hardened heart, ossified after years of fighting the endless battle of Humanity vs. Household Insect, if it hadn't been for the circumstances.

This same child made a huge fuss once because I inadvertently stood on a beetle on the step. As if I *meant* to stand on the bloody beetle!

And here was the big one. One day Lou rescued a frog she found under the sofa. Why was she looking there? God knows. Determined to save it from a terrible death by dehydration in the sofa dust, she toddled through the kitchen with it clutched in her chubby little hand.

Unfortunately, Sweetie Pie, the duck, was at the back door amusing herself pooing on the coir mat while waiting for a person to appear so she could hiss at them and hound them for food. Enter Lulu who, clutching the frog in an outstretched hand, paused at the door and turned her head for a moment to explain her mission. In a flash, Sweetie Pie leapt up and unceremoniously snatched the frog as if it was a holy offering.

A terrible struggle ensued, with much loud squawking from the duck and bellowing from the child and dreadful frog noises from the frog, which was very soon the length of a medium adult shoe and horribly, horribly inert as it slid ignominiously down Sweetie Pie's long neck, one green foot waving a tragic farewell.

Lou was inconsolable. The whole family, in fact, who had witnessed this distressing spectacle from the breakfast table, was badly shaken.

The episode did not, however, dent Lou's love of defenceless creatures. So passionate was she that vermin control was a nightmare. We had to hide mouse traps, and empty them under cover of darkness.

In the case of the toilet fly, I eventually managed to convince her that hygiene had greater priority than rescuing flies from ignoble places.

I do believe that even a card-carrying Advocate for Animals would stop short of fishing a fly out of the toilet with a dessertspoon. Especially one taken from and returned to the kitchen drawer.

THIRTY-FIVE

Crossing the Mothering Divide

We have ways and means, we mothers. Hanging out the washing in the back yard is just one of mine; a daily task and, to be frank, a rather welcome respite. It's one of my ways and means—and I work it fully.

I hide behind the sheets, see. If I keep very quiet out there, the kids can't find me. The world goes by on the farm, and while I commune with the clothes line, I catch a glimpse of other lives and routines. Animal ones. And it helps me to get things in perspective.

The dogs keep me company, the mother dog often hiding with me behind the sheets to retreat from her demanding babies. The birds in the aviary chatter and squabble in a comforting and oddly familiar way. Every now and then a chook lays an egg to a triumphant chorus of barnyard cackling. Up in the gum tree near the stables, the baby galahs squawk and screech, the same repetitive sound over and over and over again. It drives me nuts; this must surely be what compels their mothers to unforeseen and urgent tasks well out of sight and earshot also.

And the mickey birds, well, they just dart down and try to steal my pegs. But I don't really mind. As long as they keep my secret, I can spare a few pegs.

So I dream away, the cacophony from all those other species, functioning or dysfunctioning, like music to my ears. Oh yes, it's peaceful alright. If someone bellows, "Marm," I choose engagement or anonymity as the mood takes me. It works till my feet are discovered protruding beneath the wet sheets. That's as much freedom as I can ask for while my kids are young, and I take what I can get.

So there I was one time, being discreet, with not a lot on my mind and a satisfyingly large (due to school holidays) basketful of washing to string out.

Suddenly, my peace was interrupted by our three-month-old thoroughbred foal that lives in the paddock over the back fence, calling anxiously for his mum.

The mother did not reply.

"Mum! Mum!!" he whinnied with more urgency. Still no answer. I started to get anxious. Where was the mare? Had she got out and, like the colt from Old Regret, run off with the wild bush horses, leaving us to poddy her bereft foal? Was this another horse drama unfolding, involving barbed wire and spurting blood and gore, and only a moment left until the spark of life dimmed in her struggling form, with only me here to save her?

Living around these flighty creatures, you soon learn about their talent for drama and disaster.

The foal was now running up and down, calling and

calling. Where the hell was she? Why didn't she respond to her baby, being, after all, a dumb animal with powerful mothering instincts essential for the survival of her species, unlike us sophisticated humans who have choices?

My heart pounding, I abandoned the washing to go in search of her. I spotted her straight away.

There she was, hiding (can you believe it? bloody hiding!) behind a low branch of the pepperina tree up the back. She kept her head almost at ground level because the pepperina leaves obstructed her view, and she was slyly watching her baby grow more frantic by the minute as he searched for her. And yet, she remained silent. I could almost detect a smug grin on her aristocratic lips.

One call from her—just one—would have ended the drama; but no. She chose not. Gobsmacked, I watched as she very deliberately stayed shtum, just watching. Hiding, as it were, behind the sheets. And she stayed like that for about five minutes. That's a long time to a baby, and to an anxious observer too. In the end, the foal was in a real state, running in crazy circles, squealing in genuine distress, and about to do something really silly. This was a valuable foal. "Hey, lady," I yelled to myself, "I get your drift—but hasn't this gone far enough?"

Then just when the foal reached the point of hysteria, it happened. With a soft snicker, the mother ended her silence. She called out to him, and in an instant, it was over.

As the foal suckled peacefully, for all the world a tough guy again, I returned to my washing line. Another mother had joined the mother's club. Different species, yes, but the same set of priorities.

We have our ways and means, we mothers.

THIRTY-SIX

Being Rubbished

Rubbish disposal always gets me down in the dumps. We are too far out of town to qualify for a wheelie bin, yet too close to town and on too small an acreage to have our own rubbish pit discreetly secreted way out in the back paddock.

So the rubbish accumulates until eventually the dog gets into the overflow and spreads it around the yard, and something has to be done. Usually by Mother.

It was therefore with great interest and appreciation that I read the notice from kindy that said, "Please bring in all recyclable household rubbish."

You know, there may have been more to that notice, I don't know. I am usually in a hurry, and quite frankly, that was enough for me. "Please bring in all recyclable household rubbish" was all I saw at a glance, and it sounded fantastic. Whoopee!

"What an excellent fund-raising idea," I mused, not

exactly altruistically, to no one in particular. Anything to save a trip to the dump. "And," I added sagely, nodding at the kids, who of course were not listening, "children and parents alike will learn about the value of recycling."

So that week we saved up the cornflakes packet, two toilet roll innards, and the milk cartons, carefully rinsed, and rather smugly popped them into the kindy recycling receptacle. Hooray! One less trip to the dump. Everyone was happy about that. Well, I was. It didn't actually make much difference to anyone else.

The next week though, when I went to pick up my darling cherub from kindy, she disappeared to collect her art works as usual and came back proudly bearing two artistic creations made from—wait for it—our cornflakes packet, plus several other cereal packets from other people's homes, plus more toilet roll innards than we had deposited, a milk carton (unwashed) AND a fruit juice carton, a cordial bottle, an old paper plate (used, I am sure), and some silver paper.

The fact is, I often have the uncomfortable sensation that everyone else knows something I do not. It could have something to do with being too impatient to read notices all the way through, or browse internet sites, and all that sort of boring detail. This, then, was one of those blinding moments. The thing was, NO ONE ELSE LOOKED SURPRISED OR AGITATED as their children humped everyone else's rubbish out to their cars! What did they know that I did not? How could this possibly be okay? How come no-one else looked even baffled, or even mildly put out, by this astonishing and unexpected turn of events?

Should I perhaps have read that notice right to the end?

Or was this, in fact, a plot organised by the parents of uncreative children to save themselves trips to the dump?

"Look what I made, Mummy!"

Look? I had trouble shutting my mouth, let alone my eyes. This was going to take several trips just to put it in the car, and then have to be displayed in a prominent place once we got home.

My mind went straight into overdrive assessing all the implications: the kindy year had just begun; there is only so much display space on the kitchen shelf—in fact, in our entire home; and where was I going to put this stuff? Were we going to be able to get into our home by the end of the kindy year? How was I going to put the requisite positive slant on this shocking development so as not to dent my child's delicate, evolving self-esteem?

My therapist would have been proud of me. I pulled myself together, breathing evenly and deeply, artfully arranged my lips into a ghastly smile and said with heartfelt insincerity, "Wow!

THIRTY-SEVEN

First Day

For a long time, school was a safely distant spectre for Sam. First there was Christmas, then his sixth birthday, then a holiday in Melbourne. People kept asking him about school and he would say, "Yes, I'm going to school. Isn't that a nice bird/interesting insect/cool picture over there? We've got some puppies. Isn't it hot? We're going for a swim later. We went to Melbourne in a jet ..." until they safely lost interest and changed the subject.

Then suddenly all that was in the past and it was time to buy the uniform, sew on name tags, get out the book list, cover the books, name the brand new pencils and pens. There were many discussions to allay fears about who would be there, who he would know, how nice the teacher is, how like Preschool it would be. How life would go on.

With just a couple of sleeps to go, nonchalant on the outside, he was obviously clutching at straws on the inside. "Mum," he said one day, in a moment of brilliance, reprieve written all over his face. "Do you think you could get a job as a teacher and then send me to the school where you work?"

"Not in the next two days, sweetheart."

More signs of imminence when the lunch box is brought out of the cupboard and the new water bottle scoured. Then that evening, the water bottle is filled with water and put in the freezer. "School tomorrow," says Mum.

At bedtime, desperation-driven, under cover of darkness, a small boy says to his mother, "Mum, have you got any Brave Tablets?"

We both know what they are for. "As a matter of fact, yes, I have," says Mum. And sure enough next morning, after Dad has given the new boots a final touch-up with the polish, his new lunch box packed, books stowed in the shiny new school port, Mum brings out a small brown bottle labelled (freshly, if the truth be known) *"Brave Tablets. Take One as Needed. Or More if Absolutely Necessary."*

In it are six oblong white tablets, smelling suspiciously of peppermint. "They look just like Tic Tacs," says Mum. "They smell just like Tic Tacs too," says Sam.

Dad brings out a Northern Territory stick pin, which has suddenly morphed into a lucky stick pin, and with some ceremony, he attaches it to the school backpack. "If you feel sad, touch this and remember that we love you."

The Brave Tablets are safely tucked into the front pouch. "You'll be right," says Dad. "I know," says Sam, "I have some Brave Tablets."

Goodbyes all round, and a happy, relaxed little boy strides out of the house, smiling, confident in the knowledge that he has a secret weapon.

"I'll give one to William. I know he will be feeling very nervous."

The closer we get to school, the more rigid the smile becomes. The glowing cheeks start to whiten, and all the while, the mother chats on. "If I need a tablet," says Sam, "I'll just hold the bottle. Their power will come through the bottle. Won't it, Mum?"

Break my heart with your innocence, cherub! Would that it could. "Of course it will."

Across the road, through the schoolyard, and up the steps we tramp, each with a firmer than necessary grip on the other's hand. If his stomach is churning half as much as mine … poor little mite. Now I can't look at him; I have to keep on top of this. I never realised *I'd* be a problem. Pity I gave him only six of those tablets. I could really do with half a dozen or so myself right now.

"Mum, can you stay beside me? Please, Mum. Just for a little bit longer?" Well, the answer is no. I have picked up the note of despair in the tremulous little voice; Mum is feeling decidedly out of sorts. I don't think Mrs Keevers needs a large blubbering tub of lard in the middle of her classroom.

With a final, throttled "Bye bye, darling, Mummy loves you," she hurtles out, choking back the stream of tears threatening to erupt inappropriately in public.

Not just because of the sentimentality, but because she has taken a quick peek and seen the brave little face—trembling lips desperately sucking on a Brave Tablet, pale cheeks, panic-stricken eyes to be etched forever on her memory; and above all, the knowledge of the stoic determination to survive, that makes him sit there among strangers, clasping his little bottle of Brave Tablets instead of following his instinct and breaking from the ranks to chase after the safe figure of his dear, disappearing old Mum.

In the safety of the car, trembling hands reach into a battered handbag for the Tic Tacs. The tears begin to fall as not one, not two but a handful of Brave Tablets fall out and are stuffed between quivering lips.

Take one as needed. Or more if absolutely necessary.

THIRTY-EIGHT

First Day —Last Day

Aeons ago now, or so it seems, I wrote a story that resonated with mothers of Year One students everywhere.

It was about that morning, 12 long years ago, when I took my little boy Sam, my firstborn, to school for the first time.

Yes, I put on a brave face, and so did my little boy. Together we marched into the schoolyard—late, as it turned out, since, being greenhorns in the matter of schooling, we went in the wrong gate and got hopelessly lost somewhere in the teachers' car park.

This didn't help matters.

We had left our arrival at that imposing edifice till the last possible moment. The plan was to limit that dreadful moment of parting. But getting lost was not part of the plan.

Oh, will I ever forget the look on that anxious little face! The sweating palms, both of us, as we clutched each other's hands, looking the other way, anywhere but at each other. It wasn't just near-panic—it was absolute panic, for both of us. Short of breath, hearts palpitating, eyes blurred. Ah! How it wrenched my gut then, to leave my baby there alone in that classroom, his eyes full of tears and desperation following my blundering passage out of the room full of strangers.

How it wrenches my gut all these 12 years later—a lifetime!—to reread my story about his first day, and remember! And how it wrenches my gut to look at him now, a man. And to know that he is ready to move on.

So much water under the bridge as all six feet two of him gallantly—nay confidently—strides towards the last day of school. The world is at his feet, his life an open book and his education a palate of colour with which to paint his life in it! Now I look up, where once I looked down, to meet his eye. And his eye meets mine with the confidence of the man he has become. He is so eager to drink from the cup of all that life seems to hold for him in that magic world, The Future! A world that is his, not mine, where he will make a life, but not me.

How much blood, sweat and tears have gone into the making of this fine young man. Only six short years ago we had to collect him in the middle of the night from a friend's house because he was too distressed and homesick to sleep away from home. Yet the miracle of time and growth is so complete that in a couple of weeks he will fly alone across the world to Germany, to live with strangers and attend a school more literally foreign than the stuff of his nightmares a mere 12 years ago.

Who would have thought he would come so far, that anxious, shrinking little fellow who wanted his mum to get a job at his school so her familiar face would not be far away? These days he is comfortable to stand, alone and in the spotlight, on a stage to sing like an angel—albeit a baritone one—for an appreciative audience.

Now the homework he brings home, and his physics assignments, are so complex that I am lost in science after paragraph one, and looking for the diagrams so I can fudge some seemingly intelligent comment.

Now he knows stuff I will never know. Sadly, he has long since realised that I don't know so very much after all—but he's very polite about it. I had a feeling it wouldn't last, being the font of all knowledge.

But it was nice while it did.

As I prepare to bid him farewell from the home that has nurtured him for the last 18 years, I prepare to put on my brave face. Strangely, I am ready for his departure. He has outgrown us. He is ready to fly. What we haven't taught him by now, he will have to learn himself, the hard way. And while our nest will be a refuge for him to tend the wounds life will doubtless inflict upon him from time to time, this little piggy is ready to roll.

Fingers crossed, he will build himself a house of bricks to keep out the wolves.

THIRTY-NINE

Jock Saves the Day

Wanted: an emergency parenting pack. Use: to help the hapless parent manage any given situation. Must be: simple to use, easy to conceal, appealing to target. Must get results.

And don't suggest Minties. Well, okay, perhaps Minties are as good as anything, provided you are armed with them at all times. And you need to be, because when you are a parent of young kids, you never know when you are going to need to pull something out of the bag.

For example: you're standing in a queue at the local service station. You are accompanied by your three darling small children and have noted with not a little anxiety that the service area is packed with bikies—Hell's Angels actually—on their way to the Bathurst 500 races. You are trying to look inconspicuous, buy your newspaper and three lollipops as quickly as possible, and get your precious babies out of there before the riot starts.

Your blonde, cherubic little daughter is taking all this in, no doubt feeling your anxious vibes as well. Suddenly she yells, "Wow look, Mum! That man's got tatts ALL OVER HIM! Aw, GROSS!" Unfortunately, he also happens to be the bloke in front of you in the queue, nothing at all wrong with his hearing. He's the original macho man, a bikie who may have merely committed a single murder for his initiation rite, although he's no doubt capable of more by the look of him. He probably has many colourful phrases in his vocabulary to describe himself, but 'gross' is most certainly not one of them.

The cherubic daughter won't shut up about the tatts and his other obvious charms. As the bikie turns slowly around and aims his menacing glare at me, I smile weakly and search my pockets frantically for the Minties. Nope, none there, despite this being a "moment like these". I decide to skip the newspaper and melt discreetly away. This, of course, becomes impossible because the kids object loudly and heartily to the abandonment of the lollipop plan. So the riot starts anyway and you realise you have caused it.

Oh, for a pocketful of Minties!

Fast forward a few weeks to a child's birthday party strategically located next to the swings in the local park opposite the police station. It's got to be the safest public place in town. Most of the kids are having an absolute ball on the swings, now and then rushing over to the table where bowls of Smarties, chips and assorted lollies fuel their darling little bodies, while the balloons keep most of them happy.

Most of them. But *my* toddler has spotted something

far more interesting than swings, lollies and balloons. Sitting tensely on a park bench just out of range of the bubble of party happiness, is the big, bad brother of that Hell's Angel—yes, the one with all the lovely tatts in the servo a few weeks before. Only *this* bloke is the black sheep of the family. He makes the whole gang at the service station look real tame. Here he is, horror of horrors, sitting on our park bench, looking like Satan himself. His precious bike is gleaming and magnificent nearby. He is disciplining one of his two bikie molls, who is cringing at the pointy end of his torrent of abuse.

Evil is written in the concentrated look of rage on his face, in the aggressive set of his muscular body, the tense pitch of the rings through his bare nipples. Oh, and there's a long hunting knife slung conspicuously from his belt.

He slaps his knife with one hand and waves the other at the terrified moll. The situation is seriously tense.

This guy is Prepared to Do Anything. Having a kid hanging about is obviously not going to improve his image.

Nonetheless, my little Jock makes a beeline for him. Not for Jock the Smarties and balloons, games and fun. With the speed of light, he bolts from the sanctuary of his mother's knee and runs to this man, gooing with the Trust of Innocence into the Aura of Malevolence.

Malevolence pauses in his tirade, and gives me the death stare as I fuss into his little axis of evil to clasp my baby to my anxious bosom.

Not once or twice but again and again Jock turns his back on the delights of innocence and returns to his new friend, a one-way relationship of astounding dimensions, while Malevolence ominously rubs his hunting knife and glares at the happy little kid and his agitated mother.

Should I offer him a Mintie?

We can't choose our kids' friends or who they hang out with. We can but try to fill them with enough love and respect for humankind that wherever they go, whatever they do, they add a little kindness to the world, in whatever guise they choose to roam.

Who knows? Jock may be a Hell's Angel himself one day. His mother always had a thing about bikes. Let's just hope she will have been able to instil in him enough good stuff to ensure that he is a bikie with a social conscience.

FORTY

Melbourne

It was the summer holidays, and Aunty Nick said please come and stay with me in Melbourne. The Old Boy couldn't come, so the kids and I packed up our summer clothes and our winter clothes, our sunscreen and our raincoats, our European and Asian language guides and off we went to Melbourne.

You have to be prepared for everything in Melbourne. It plays merry hell with the extra luggage.

Yep, off to the Big Smoke! The real Big Smoke. From our home in Warwick, it's even further away than Brisbane, that most distant of destinations. This fact is very difficult to grasp when you are very, very young. You are on the plane for less time than you are in the car on the trip to Brisbane; how can Melbourne possibly be further away?

Take my word for it—it is. When you are strapped into a confined space beside two over-excited small people, both of whom think they should be sitting in the window seat;

and when you have a small atom bomb on your knee trying to get a grip on the glasses of the bloke across the aisle—for two hours. When you discover that Sam has brought his water bottle and, very thoughtfully, tucked it head down under your bottom but has not put the lid on properly, and you become dripping wet in places it is very hard to explain away with dignity.

When you have to eat your lunch with a baby on your knee in an area the size of a small handkerchief. Then when you think that things could not get worse the baby gets that look of intense concentration on his face and you realise, yes, things could—and do—very shortly.

There's no doubt, under these circumstances, it is quite a long way to Melbourne.

However, we got there, and stayed with the glamorous Aunty Nick in very salubrious surroundings. No, thanks, we declined the offer of the use of her car in which to lose ourselves for all time. We felt we could get lost just as effectively and with less nerve-wracking effect on the public transport system.

We rode in a green tram, a red tram and a blue tram. Did we care where they were going? Heavens, no! They were trams, and each was a different colour. That was what *really* mattered.

We rode in a taxi, the greatest thrill of all (I mean, a car with a sign on the roof? Yes, but it's a *taxi*. Okay, okay, we'll go in a taxi).

The taxi driver, on being told we were from Queensland, said he had never been to the United States himself. (Which part of the galaxy did he come from?)

Yes, well, we felt as if we were in another country too.

Then to see the vista of where we had been, laid out before us in all its magnificent splendour as far as the eye could see, we went up the top of the highest building in Melbourne, the Rialto. I carried the baby. But can I suggest to you, if you want your nerve-endings frayed for all time, try shepherding two excited country kids through a revolving door! I was a wreck just keeping the extraneous bits of them intact, let alone coordinating things so that we all popped out. As it happened, we did, at the same time and in the same place. What luck!

Returning to the ground floor, and not wanting to repeat the experience with the revolving door, I surreptitiously headed for the ordinary door.

"No, no, this way, Mum," said Miss Bossy Boots. "I want to go through the disgusting door."

Revolving, revolting, disgusting—what's in a word? I wasn't too keen on that door myself.

FORTY-ONE

Chaos Effect

There once was a career woman—single and busy.
She lived an orderly life.
She had a place for everything, and everything was in its place. She didn't put a thing "down"; she put it "away". Her life was tidy. Her life was organised. Everything was "just so".

At work and at home, she was in charge, and no small detail of orderliness escaped her. What she said, went. Whatever she did was as close to "spot on" as she could make it.

This woman had no time for trivia, no time for nonsense. No time to spare.

Does she sound familiar?

Oh, yes! Dinner guests had their plates whisked off to the sink with super efficiency before their last mouthful had been swallowed; the plates were scrubbed in a flash and replaced on the shelf in colour coordinated rows between meal courses. The courses were delivered with style and panache, the menu carefully planned and perfectly executed.

This woman (and dare you to have been the one to tell her so) was typical of many career-minded, hyperactive women: organised, efficient, adrenaline-powered, and in control.

Still, a heart was beating in there, and she could not suppress a secret dream—marriage, a house in the country, a few kids. Some chooks, a garden, a family dog, and a horse or two out the back.

Time passed, and the tempo of life had changed. It was with a sudden sense of wonder that this woman realised she had arrived in her dream. She had left her run a bit late but Prince Charming, at 42, though a little shop-soiled, was unused. The kids started arriving, and were textbook cases, like most kids are. But, which career-minded single female has had access to such textbooks? These, she had desperately pounded the pavements to acquire when she realised she was alone on the shifting sands of motherhood, in sole charge of these terrifying, uncontrollable, unpredictable small morsels of humanity.

More time passed. Her life had moved into a different dimension altogether. Disorderliness had become the norm. It was quite standard for dirty teaspoons to be popped back into drawers because "I only had a tiny bit of Milo, Mum." Slimy wet things and sharp-edged square things—all sorts of things, in fact—lay on the floor around the house, in wait for unsuspecting bare feet. Doors were left open that should have been shut; doors were shut that should have been left open. Items of small clothing were discarded and replaced several times throughout the day. The dirty washing pile grew and grew, and was always out of hand. The clean washing pile grew and grew, and was always out of hand.

Orders were not necessarily obeyed.

The changes had happened over a long period of time, in a blur of confusion, exhaustion and joy; but this erstwhile orderly woman knew she had arrived somewhere different altogether, upon rushing home from a post-work grocery shopping expedition one day, eagerly anticipating her first solo excursion in over a year—albeit a girls' night out at a local art show opening. Prince Charming had agreed to babysit (sole charge was not his forte).

The woman was thinking that after a refreshing hot shower, she might splurge the dregs of the French perfume for the occasion. She was wondering what clothes might fit her new body, mangled by childbearing, and whether the bouffant hairstyle would be the most appropriate or perhaps something a little bohemian to suit the arty-farty company.

She did not stop to consider how times had changed, or how strange it was that the prospect of a simple outing should fill her with such disproportionate joy. She hastily put the groceries away and rushed headlong into the hallway while there was still a little spare time to luxuriate in a leisurely shower.

With a blinding flash, a lightbulb moment you could call it, she saw how her life had truly changed. For in the middle of the hallway, outside the bathroom, was a small but action-packed scene.

Prince Charming, frantic, was on his hands and knees on the sodden carpet. An excited small son hopped around him offering advice and consolation. They had saturated every towel in the house in a futile attempt to soak up the entire contents of the hot water system. And with it, my shower dream—which now flowed sluggishly through the steaming shagpile carpet and down the hallway.

The bath had been left running, apparently. More important things—well, games in the garden—were going on. Everyone forgot about the bath, Mum. ALL the hot water has come out! There's none left. How about that!

How about that, indeed.

And what did she do?

Ah, but how the years had mellowed her! She merely phoned the carpet man, joined in the chain gang wringing out towels, settled for dirty hair and a pat under the arms with some talcum, and went off looking bohemian anyway and decidedly unwashed. As it turned out, the theme for the night was Medieval.

Yes. I know about all this. Because, of course, that woman was me.

FORTY-TWO

Confessions of an Easter Bunny

I don't often sit up late these days, but there are times when duty calls. And Easter Saturday is one of them. Stoically I sit, bleary-eyed as the hours chime by, pleased to be a woman with a mission. I will get to lay down my weary bones well past my customary 8.30 bed time. Meanwhile, the Old Boy snores in comfortable fatherly fashion in his chair, as is his wont, with not a care in his world. Mum must stay alert and on duty to attend to the essential business of the night.

My mission is, I suspect, one which is commonly left to mothers. It is two-fold. The first part is to deliver a letter to the Easter bunny, which says, "*Dear Ester Buni, We lov you. Ples giv uss lots uv egs. Luv, The Grieve Kids.*"

The second part requires me to stay awake longer than the Grieve kids. Three hope-filled baskets have been stationed in places deemed to be inaccessible to mice and other vermin (such as early rising baby brothers). It is my job to load them up with what I hope will be just the right number of Easter eggs; just enough to avoid disappointment, and few enough to avoid creating unreasonable future expectations, hyperglycaemia, hyperactivity and (heaven forbid!) spoiling.

I am acutely aware of how easily things can go wrong. Last Easter Saturday evening I became distracted by fatigue and routine ablutions, and what with one thing leading to another as per my usual evening ritual, I almost forgot my obligations. By sheer luck, this did not happen. Having tucked myself up for a good night's sleep with an uncomfortable, "I'm sure there's something I've forgotten to do" feeling, just before I dropped off to sleep, one Grieve kid called me from his bed with more public relations instructions for the comfort, flattery and general seduction of the Easter bunny. Ye Gods, that's right, I remembered and, leaping out of bed, I returned to my post. Waiting, weary.

Tonight as I strive to keep my eyes open, long-gone Easters float through my tenuous consciousness. I just love the tradition of the Easter bunny. I love the way the generations are bonded by the common threads of this precious ritual. Memories are made of these times.

One childhood memory that this night brings to my mind is the Easter when we stayed with our neighbours, the Freshneys and the big kids, now glamorous society ladies, got into the baskets before we small kids were awake, and had their way with all the best eggs. We wondered how their mother knew to scold them and redistribute them. We hadn't noticed anything untoward. We thought the Easter bunny did us proud at the Freshneys' place.

Funny thing, they only lived on the next door farm but we couldn't help noticing that his Reverence the Bunny brought them much grander Easter eggs than he had ever brought us. We wondered whether, had we been at home that year, our eggs may also have been more up-market—perhaps he had engaged a more imaginative cook? The most unforgettable one, and I can see it plainly after more years than I care to mention, was a beautiful egg made of pure spun sugar. It was a dentist's delight, so delicate that we knew it must have been made by fairies.

How did we ever keep our teeth? In those days, you didn't get chocolate eggs, just huge sugar eggs (with a surprise inside) through which you crunched and sucked your way for days. You had a semi-permanent coating of sugar on your teeth all that time, and got sticky stuff all over everything you touched.

We kept our teeth, albeit alum-filled. And with the highly sophisticated dental techniques available these days, I assume a one-off attack of chocolate tomorrow will not ruin my kids' chances of keeping theirs. It's me I'm worried about. I need my sleep. How am I going to get three excited Grieve kids to go to sleep before midnight?

FORTY-THREE

Second Time Around

I am living testimony to the fact that life is a treadmill. I don't mind that. But lately I have found that it is actually a round treadmill, and I am on my second circle.

This is how it goes.

You're born. Everyone loves everything you do.

You turn into a child, scorn the behaviour of babies, do puerile, stupid things and get some sense knocked into you one way or another.

Then you turn into an adolescent, scorn the behaviour of children, do more puerile, stupid things and have more sense knocked into you.

At last, you turn into an adult. Naturally, you scorn the behaviour of adolescents, and have learned by now to do your puerile and stupid things discreetly. You get away with them because all the other adults are doing them too and have an unwritten conspiracy of silence.

Then you become a parent! Willy nilly you are thrown

back into the first part of the cycle. Your capacity for doing puerile, stupid things is by now tenfold, due largely to size and years of furtive practice. One difference however—you are now forced out into the open.

So one day Lou comes in and says, "Sam has just poured Coke into your slipper."

"No tales now," say I sanctimoniously, but on reflection I decide that this is something that should be dealt with. This on its own would be a manageable occurrence. Sam and I get on well. I know it's not because he has a vendetta of some kind against me. He likes me. It's just because he wants to see if the Coke will make the wool go black, or leak onto the carpet and make it go black too. Or perhaps there is not a cup in the room and he wants a drinking utensil? Who knows? He's a healthy, inquisitive six-year-old, and he didn't expect his little sister to go telling the owner of the slipper that it had been the subject of a scientific experiment.

For sure, he also thought that I wouldn't notice Coke in my slipper, since I usually rush around in the mornings with a glazed and vacuous expression on my face, appearing not to notice much at all.

Life will go on as usual, he no doubt reasoned.

But of course, to me there are other issues: like that everything I own has had Coke poured into it just for an experiment; or bits pulled off; or been carted up to the shed and beaten with a hammer to see if it will break; or taken to show and tell without my knowledge and left at Preschool.

Or tucked away in someone's money box.

And the house is a mess of children's things and I am

trying to get myself and three other human beings ready for the day and I am feeling, to put it bluntly, fractious.

Besides, I don't want Coke in my slipper. There is always that insignificant little point. Suddenly it's just one thing too many.

Now, a psychologist would say, "Speak gently but firmly with the child. Explain why this was not an appropriate thing to do at 8.30 on a workday morning; say, 'Would you like it if someone put Coke in *your* slipper, Sam dear?'"

Yeah, yeah, I've read all the books.

"And," he would add, "make sure the child knows you love him and approve of him, but disapprove of what he has done …"

So. Who has time for that at 8.30 on a workday morning?

"Sam, c'm'ere, and bring your new joggers and the Coke bottle." (Glugging sounds) "There, how do you like that? Now go and get ready for Preschool."

The morning dissolves into total, instead of partial chaos. Sam is shocked and heartbroken because I put Coke in one of his new joggers! He is absolutely astounded! Positively affronted! Can you believe it? The fact that he put Coke in *my* slipper has nothing to do with it, nothing at all! I am a mother; mothers are supposed to tolerate these small inconveniences in the name of science.

Hey listen, all you child psychologists—I love yez. You've been my lifeline these six years. Here's an invitation for you. Come to our place at 8.30 next workday morning and keep a benevolent, unselfish, tolerant and understanding eye on the kids, will you? And while you're here, can you just make the beds, cook a bit of breakfast, do the washing up, sweep the kitchen floor, get the mice out of the traps, change the baby's dirty nappy, supervise the kids' dressing, feed the dogs, cut the lunches, and tip the Coke out of my slipper, while I get ready for work?

What? Too busy writing? Oh, pity, that!

FORTY-FOUR

A Brush with Danger

There was a very long period in my life, once I had at last reached that glorious mountaintop of adulthood, when I could say with absolute confidence that no-one else in the entire world had ever used my toothbrush.

You know—even before that time, back in the Dark Ages when I was a kid myself, I thought that was quite a reasonable belief to hold close to my heart. Anyway, I doubt whether anyone in my family of origin was slightly interested in using my toothbrush. It just wasn't part of our family culture. And I guess, to be honest, they may have been within their rights to wonder where it had been.

I was once so insular that I may very well have thrown up if I thought my toothbrush had been used for anything else, by anyone else. Precious, I was in those days, just precious. Because while I am on the mat I will admit that, so obsessive and determined was I about the one-person-one-toothbrush concept, I have in the past bought myself a NEW toothbrush rather than use one that I suspected had been anywhere, anywhere at all, but in MY mouth and MY toothmug at MY behest. There! I've said it.

Halcyon days those were. It never occurred to me to wonder if this was an abnormal fixation. I just felt that toothbrushes were absolutely personal accoutrements, to be used by one person only, ever, for the life of the toothbrush. Pretty simple really. This far-off concept still seems to me to be quite a reasonable belief, even though it has now faded into my distant memory.

The awful thing is that since the kids started being independent about their personal hygiene, I cannot be sure just where my toothbrush has been or what it has been doing.

It's disgusting, but I am saying here that even if the dog's teeth are extra shiny I look closely at my toothbrush that night.

And it's not just mine. There is a family precedent. One of the kids' cousins, when he was quite small, was scolded by his mother for going into Gran's house with his feet covered in mulberry stains.

"Clean your feet AT ONCE," she bellowed.

The little darling disappeared, and returned some time later with spotless feet.

That night, when Gran went into her bathroom, she found that her handbasin and handtowel were purple. So was her toothbrush!

Back in our house, I realised that something was amiss when I spotted the Old Boy's toothbrush being used in the shower with the kids. They were industriously cleaning the tile grouting, the darling little things, leaving impossible smears of soap all over the glass door.

There was quite an alarming lot of black stuff on that tile grouting, and needless to say, quite a lot of black stuff on the toothbrush too.

I have to hand it to them though. When I saw the toothbrush later, duly stashed back in the tooth-mug, it was spotless. The Old Boy didn't notice a thing.

But there's no doubt about it, toothbrushes are handy little buggers. They are so tempting, just the right size for so many uses, and kept at just the right height in a room that is not out of bounds. It's no wonder I have found our toothbrushes in so many weird and wonderful places, doing all sorts of unlikely jobs in small hands.

I can't say I like it though, even if I understand it. I indignantly reclaim those errant brushes and throw them in the rubbish bin—only to find them recovered and back in service cleaning tiny teeth before nightfall.

It's a worry. I'm sure that it's just a matter of time till Lou notices that her pony, Bluebell, has yellow teeth. I hope I'm around when she does. Then I will quickly direct her to something of a more appropriate size—say, the toilet brush. That should do the job nicely.

Epilogue

I awaken to the song of the magpies in the myall tree near my window.

Through the lifting dawn I can see that the tree has grown —my, how it's grown! The whole garden has grown. The sun in its early-morning incarnation is hard pressed to make an impression through all the shrubbery nowadays.

The red-bellied black snake that now lives under the eremophila bush nearby keeps his own counsel, and I keep mine.

The fairies in the eremophila are still asleep, no doubt. I haven't seen them for simply ages. You know, I haven't even thought of them for so long. I wonder if they are still there?

I lie back in my third of the warm bed. The Old Boy gently snores beside me, the invisible person on his other side staying shtum as usual, but taking up just as much space as always.

The magpie song lulls me like an old, familiar symphony.

It is a most beautiful melody. My eyes close again as the morning sounds wash around me.

The lovebirds in the aviary out the back, near Sam's empty room, start a tentative, discordant squawking to herald the new day. The occasional car swishes through the fog on the highway below, and a calf calls for its mother somewhere up the hill.

I hear a quick scuffle outside and know it's just a wallaby or two in the garden. They will be grazing on the lawn, I think fondly. Well, I hope they're only eating the bloody lawn. My eyes fly open; then close again.

Suddenly one of the cats starts its victory moan in the hallway. It's Spot, I know his voice. I should know it by now. He was born on Lou's ninth birthday. Spot's mother, now long gone, was her eighth birthday gift. How old does that make him—eight? Nine? My goodness! It seems like yesterday ... but you see, it WAS yesterday. Just yesterday.

Spot has caught a mouse and he is taking it to Jock's room as a love offering.

But Jock is not there. Jock's away. He lives at boarding school in Brisbane now. As I roll over, I know there will be a mouse tail, and perhaps a few whiskers, to vacuum up later. Unless the offering is a pigeon, then there will be feathers, and signs of a struggle, and a mop will be called for.

Breakfast, and it's just us. Me and the Old Boy. And an assortment of animals to feed and tend.

Our children have moved on with their lives now, leaving us living in the detritus of their childhoods.

Spot and the other cat, Teaker, mourn the kids and still deposit mice at their bedroom doors as tender offerings.

There's Shadow, my terrier dog, who is my baby now and the best mouser west of the Great Dividing Range. And Bob, the red dog, the best darn sheepdog the Old Boy's ever had. Except for PJ, Missy's dad, another kelpie. He was a pretty good shed dog. But no, for an all-rounder, Bob's the One.

There's no rooster crowing the dawn; there are no bantam hens either. Symbiotic they might have been in the garden, but oh! What a relief to be able to plant seedlings and know they will still be there next week!

If the kangaroos don't eat them.

The foxes got the bantams in the end. The foxes got the guinea fowl too. It's quiet without the guinea fowl, and they would have chased the black snake away. Good thing really if they had.

You know, what it's quiet without, and I mean really, really quiet? It's quiet without the kids.

PS: 9 ante portas

Women reach a particular age and stage.

Call it what you will, but there comes a point—a tipping point, perhaps—when the years of giving come to an abrupt and rather shocking halt.

Suddenly! Behind you is the complicated topography of motherhood, with all its hills and valleys and forests and pathways and obscure places. You realise with a kind of jolt that you have managed to navigate your way, somehow, through those endless, exhilarating years of mixed degrees of blessing.

Before you now is a vista of a different sort; a vast empty plain, under an infinite, cloudless sky.

Fear not! For this is the Plain of Possibilities. At its edge stands the Crucible of Choices, bubbling away, cauldron-like, tended by a hooded crone wielding an enormous wooden spoon, her lips pursed around what appears to be a mournful dirge.

But take courage and draw closer. You will see that it's not an old woman at all; it is your former self, albeit in a new, slightly used and rather shop-soiled form. And far from chanting horrible incantations, you are whistling in a rather jaunty and not entirely dignified way, and not altogether discreetly, either.

And what is boiling in that big pot that so engages your rapt attention?

Aha! That is YOUR call. To the sum total of all you have become through your life's experiences you are free to add whatever you like! It's time to take stock, before you embark upon a journey of a different kind.

And so, in July 2008 a group of women friends of long

standing (very long standing, in fact—friendships going back generations, in the Queensland way) and at that particular stage of their lives, found themselves at a wake together, celebrating the illustrious life of the husband of one of their number.

Suse, the Widow, was a talented but unrequited artist. She had lost her lover and muse, Ulf. As she circulated, stunned by her sudden entry into that private world of grief, her friends Chrissie and Susan held a landmark conversation over the champagne and canapés.

Susan confided her decision to resume a latent talent, held over during many years of motherhood, duty, love and obligation, and become the Great Artist her childhood art teacher had said she could be. Already, a little over a year since she had begun her journey, she was well on the way.

Chrissie, a mover and shaker of a lifetime's practice, offered her moral support and further, she declared that a date must be set for an exhibition of Susan's burgeoning endeavours.

"And while we are at it," she enthused, "what could be a better way to encourage the Widow to bring her light out from under the bushel and honour Ulf's ambitions for her at the same exhibition!"

"And look," she added, a rather feverish light by now burning in her eyes, "there are one or two other women amongst us who are on the cusp of greatness, and need just a little nudge into the limelight to throw off their cloaks of self-doubt and rise to new opportunities in grand and colourful style."

And so, out of death, was the art group *9 ante portas* born.

Because surely, having gone the hard yards as had Hannibal when he arrived at the gates of Rome, there is no better time for nine talented women to throw off their shrouds of anonymity. Step gloriously up into the light now, girls, and showcase the talents that have lain dormant during all those years of motherhood, duty, love and obligation.

This book is my tribute to mothers everywhere, and in particular to my fellow 9 *ante portas* ladies, as we stand before the gates to the Plain of Possibilities. To our Fearless Leader, photographer Chrissie Higgins; to artists Susie Shaw (Ulf's widow), Susan McConnel, Heather Moore, Binnie Donovan, Peta (PeeWee) Trude; photographer Kacie Lord; and writer and mystery exhibitor Rob Skerrett.

And to Jay Bryant, an erstwhile 9 *ante portas* lady whose duty, love and obligation hold her yet in their thrall—but not forever.

May the sun forever shine in your faces, may the wind be always at your backs.

Bookmark our website, *9anteportas.com.au*, look out for us on the road and be sure to come to our Annual Art Exhibition in Brisbane.

The Muse

A group of nine women artists credits the genesis of their first art exhibition under the group name of 9 *ante portas* to the encouragement of a dear departed friend.

At the wake of Dr Ulf Sundhaussen in July 2008, the women resolved to honour his memory by supporting Diabetes Australia – Queensland through an exhibition of their combined art. Ulf was a scholar, teacher and writer, known and respected internationally and in Australia where he was an associate professor lecturing in political science at the University of Queensland.

His widow, Susie Shaw, says, "Ulf's life was about encouraging people to achieve their utmost. He always challenged people to push the boundaries of their potential.

"Now, a year after his death from diabetes-related illness, we have indeed pushed our boundaries and will honour Ulf's memory through our Exhibition at Gallery 54, Latrobe Terrace in Paddington, Brisbane, Queensland.

"Ulf was in the habit of throwing down the gauntlet to encourage endeavour. He would say, 'Think how it will feel when you have worked hard and enjoyed success. So—just get on with it!' " says Susie.

And it is in this spirit that nine women, each with a fascinating individual story, and many touched indirectly by diabetes, will express those stories through what they intend to be an annual exhibition of their art, which may well take to the road, and most certainly can be purchased online through *9anteportas.com.au*

My bit for Diabetes

Type 2 diabetes is an insidious disease.

It sneaks up on you and has its way with your organs, sometimes for years before you realise you have been carrying it around.

And here's the rub: at this stage (and not for the want of looking) there is no cure, only a management strategy—which is, to put it bluntly, manageable, but a bit of a pain.

And just quietly, you need to make sure you get to it in time. Remain vigilant, says Diabetes Australia – Queensland, because an awful lot can have gone wrong with you while you are wondering why you are peeing all the time, or heaving yourself around like a sodden wheat bag with blurry vision and aching legs, and sore bits that don't heal. Basically, why you are suddenly feeling worn out and generally dysfunctional well before your 110th birthday.

It is understandable that you might wail, *"Why me? How came I by this small disaster?"* Well, while type 1 diabetes is an unavoidable autoimmune disease, the possibility of type 2 diabetes was written in your genes. But that was the possibility only. Chances are that you have been doing things your mother told you not to; and worse, not doing things your mother told you to do. Like being a teensy, weensy little bit overweight? Not eating your greens, perhaps? Having too many Friday nights on too many nights not called Friday? Sitting about doing important things, when taking Fido for a walk in the fresh air is the thing your body (and Fido) really needed you to be doing for at least a small part of every day?

They call it "unhealthy lifestyle" at Diabetes Australia - Queensland. They say type 2 diabetes is "highly preventable" —not judgmentally, mind you, but just matter-of-fact sorta thing. Leave it to your mother to say, "I told you so!"

If you DO get diabetes (and believe me, you will not be alone; about 50 cases come to light EVERY DAY in Queensland!) Diabetes Australia - Queensland is right there at the end of the phone, talking you gently through your shock—confusion—fear—anxiety, and pointing you firmly in the right direction while they do their damnedest to find a cure.

Phew!

5% of the profits from the sale of this book will be donated to Diabetes Australia - Queensland

---

diabetesqld.org.au
1300 136 588

Jane Grieve was a career woman, having been actively engaged in the establishment of the Australian Stockman's Hall of Fame at Longreach, Queensland, Australia, as its executive director up until the birth of her first child Sam when she was 36 years old.

Her childhood being a dim memory, it was no small feat to move from suits, travel, a certain amount of glamour and being in charge of things to the shifting sands of motherhood—a world of being housebound, dressed in whatever, and then only if time allowed, and wondering, quite frankly, just who was in charge.

Sam was followed in quite quick succession by Lou, then Jock. These then are the stories of Sam, Lou, Jock and the myriad household pets, welcome and unwelcome, that attend the raising of children. On acreage, as if that made much difference.

These stories will ring bells of truth for those in the thick of it, and memory for those who have survived. Jane hopes they will make you laugh and cry as being the mother of Sam, Lou and Jock enriched her life through both laughter and tears.

www.ingramcontent.com/pod-product-compliance
Lightning Source LLC
Chambersburg PA
CBHW031225170426
43191CB00030B/216